STRIPY BLANKETS TO CROCHET

S T R I P Y
B L A N K E T S
T O C R O C H E T

20 gorgeous designs with easy repeat patterns

Haafner Linssen

Search Press

A QUARTO BOOK

Published in 2018 by
Search Press
Wellwood
North Farm Road
Tunbridge Wells
Kent TN2 3DR

Reprinted 2019 (twice), 2021

ISBN 978-1-78221-631-5

Conceived, edited and designed by
Quarto Publishing plc
an imprint of The Quarto Group
The Old Brewery
6 Blundell Street
London N7 9BH
www.quartoknows.com

QUAR STBL

Editor: Michelle Pickering
Art editor: Jacqueline Palmer
Designer: Grand Union Design
Photographers: Haafner Linssen (all except borders),
Phil Wilkins (borders)
Illustrator: Kuo Kang Chen
Pattern checker: KJ Hay
Editorial assistants: Cassie Lawrence, Danielle Watt
Publisher: Samantha Warrington

Printed in China

CONTENTS

ABOUT THIS BOOK

The book is divided into three chapters. Chapter 1 includes 20 beautiful blanket designs, plus some additional borders. Chapter 2 features a selection of projects that demonstrate how easy it is to upsize or downsize the blankets to create other types of projects. Chapter 3 provides all the technical know-how you will need to make the blankets, from changing stripe colours to working the basic stitches.

TECHNIQUES (PAGES 114–125)

Here you will find essential pattern notes that will help you understand the written patterns and charts in this book. There is also a concise summary of all the crochet stitches and techniques used to make the blankets, plus advice on choosing colours and adapting the designs. At the end of the chapter (page 126), you will find a list of the exact yarn brands and colours used to make the blankets.

PROJECTS (PAGES 102–113)

This chapter contains a selection of projects as inspiration for adapting the blanket patterns to make other items. If you want to upsize a blanket pattern, we have got you covered with a gorgeous rug and bedspread. If you want to downsize a pattern, here you will find a beautiful potholder, dish towel, cushion and wall hanging. There really is no limit to what you can do with the patterns, other than your imagination.

READ THIS FIRST!

We have strived to make the written patterns and charts in this book as simple and clear as possible, but we strongly recommend that you turn to page 118 and read the pattern notes before making your first blanket. There you will find detailed information that will help you follow the patterns and charts successfully, including how to change colours when working the stripes and a list of the abbreviations used in the patterns. As much as you might want to dive straight into the tempting blanket designs, spending a little time reading this information will pay dividends when you do pick up your yarn and hook, even if you are an experienced crocheter.

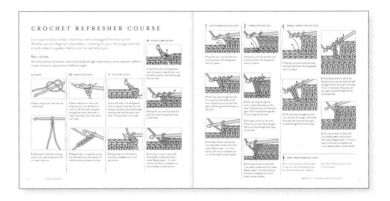

BLANKETS AND BORDERS (PAGES 10–101)

This chapter forms the heart of the book. Here you will find the 20 blanket designs, each with written instructions, crochet charts and a beautifully photographed finished example. Some of the blankets include borders as part of the design, but as a bonus you will find a selection of border patterns at the end of the chapter.

The sizes of the blankets vary slightly depending on the stitch pattern, but most are approx. 80 x 100cm (32 x 40in) to make it easier for you to compare them. The size listed at the beginning of each design is for the blanket shown in the photographs, made using the length of foundation chain specified in the written pattern.

Tips are provided to help you get the best results, and to give you ideas for some simple adaptations.

Each blanket is graded with a skill level: easy, intermediate or advanced. If you are new to crochet, try one of the easy blankets first.

The list of yarns, colours and quantities are for the size of blanket shown in the photographs. See page 126 for a list of the specific yarn brands and colours if you want to match the blanket shown exactly.

Note that the hook size used to make the blanket may be different from the usual size for a particular weight of yarn, in order to create a blanket with the required texture and drape using a particular stitch pattern.

Each blanket has its own written pattern. See page 118 for guidance on understanding the patterns.

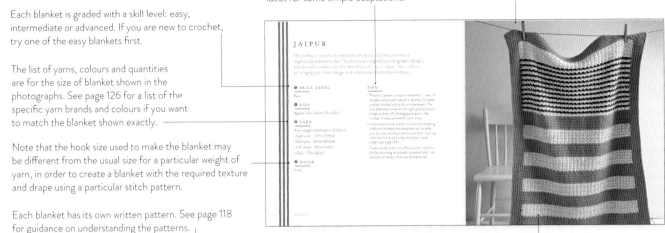

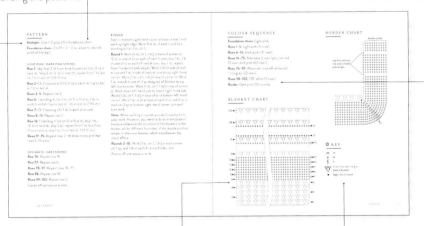

Each written pattern begins with the 'multiple' of stitches required for that blanket, so that you can easily upsize or downsize it, followed by the number of foundation chains required for the size of blanket shown in the photographs. See page 118 for more information.

Beautiful photographs show you the finished blanket, often with close-up details.

The colour sequence used for the stripes is provided separately from the pattern instructions. This is because you don't always change colour in the same place throughout the pattern, plus once you have got into the rhythm of the stitch pattern, you can refer to this listing to check when to change colour without having to search through the pattern instructions. It is also handy to have this information listed separately if you want to change the colour sequence.

Charts are provided for each blanket and border, showing all the necessary stitch repeats and rows to make the design.

A key to all of the symbols used in the charts is provided for each blanket. Check out the crochet techniques on page 120 if you need a reminder on how to perform them.

MEET HAAFNER

As a maker, you know that inspiration can be drawn from everywhere around you – nature, books, colours, architecture, even a beam of light. The blankets in this book were inspired by cities and towns around the world, by their shapes, colours and traditions, or simply by my memories of them.

You will find this reflected in the title of each blanket. In some cases there is a direct connection to the city. The Marrakech blanket, for example, was inspired by the stunning boucherouite rugs of Morocco. In other cases, the colours of a city were my inspiration, such as the Jaipur blanket, named after the stunning pink Indian city, or the mint colour of the Lisbon blanket, which is reminiscent of the city's breathtakingly pretty pastels. The Bruges blanket is my way of honouring the lace traditions and artisans of the charming Belgian town. The chevron stripes and colours of the St George's blanket reminded me of the beaches and bright sun in the capital of the delightful island of Grenada; the Tokyo blanket evoked the highrises in that energetic city. In other cases the connection is a much looser or more personal one. The Istanbul blanket, for instance, reminds me of another textured pattern I was making during a stay there.

Reading this book – and making these patterns – will hopefully feel a bit like we are travelling this amazing and beautiful world together, and I hope that your blanket will carry your own personal inspiration, memories and emotions.

I put a lot of love into making this book. I hope you will love the result.

Happy crocheting

Haafner

PS: Are you on social media? Wonderful. I would love to meet you there and see your work. Just use #joyinrepetitioncrochet. See you there.

EARN YOUR STRIPES: JOY IN REPETITION!

It is safe to say that most people love stripes. The fascinating history of stripes in design is proof of that. Some stripes are so distinctive that they have even got their own name – think Breton stripes (alternating wide white and narrow marine blue stripes) and Missoni stripes (multicoloured chevrons).

When it comes to crochet, stripe patterns have something extra going for them. Many people crochet to relax, and there is something soothing and enjoyable about a simple, repetitive pattern that builds up into something lovely – I like to call it 'joy in repetition'.

At the same time, there is an incredible variety of stripe patterns. The most basic patterns consist of a repeat of one row, but even such simple patterns can create a lovely blanket, especially with the right colours and yarn. Other patterns combine several rows but are

still relaxing patterns to make, whereas other stripe patterns can be relatively complicated and need more attention.

Many crocheters are not too fond of weaving in ends, and while a stripy blanket made in several colours does involve multiple ends to weave in, generally speaking the number of ends is less compared to a blanket composed of motifs. Plus, there is usually little or no joining involved. If you really don't like weaving in ends, then simply disguise them with a tassel fringe or pompom border.

In this book we have a lovely assortment of stripes for you – from solid to lacy stripes, basic to intricate, horizontal to vertical, diagonal to chevron, flat to textured, and delightfully eclectic mixtures.

After reading this book, I hope you will agree with me – there is joy in repetition!

CHAPTER 1

BLANKETS
& BORDERS

MARSEILLE

This is an easy and relaxing blanket to create – with a lovely result. This was actually the first blanket I crocheted for this book, and I made it solely with scraps of yarn that were left over from my previous book. I don't like to see beautiful yarn go to waste! The colours remind me of a calm sea, with all its stunning hues.

SKILL LEVEL

Easy

SIZE

Approx. 80 x 100cm (32 x 40in)

YARN

DK-weight cotton yarn in as many colours as you wish:

• Total quantity – 1,428m (1,560yd)

HOOK

4mm

PATTERN

Multiple: 2 sts, plus 2 for foundation chain.

Foundation chain: Ch 130 + 2 (or adapt to desired width of blanket).

Row 1: 1 dc in 2nd ch from hook and in each ch to end. (131 dc)

Row 2: Ch 2 (counts as 1 tr), skip first dc, 2 tr in next dc, *skip 1 dc, 2 tr in next dc; repeat from * to last dc, 1 tr in last dc. (132 tr)

Row 3: 1 standing tr (or ch 2) and 1 tr in first tr, skip 2 tr, *2 tr in space before next 2 tr, skip 2 tr; repeat from * to last st, 2 tr in last st.

Row 4: 1 standing tr (or ch 2) in first tr, skip 1 tr, *2 tr in space before next 2 tr, skip 2 tr; repeat from * to last 2 sts, 2 tr in space before last 2 sts, skip 1 st, 1 tr in last st.

Rows 5–112: Repeat rows 3–4.

Row 113: Ch 1 (turning ch), 1 dc in each st to end.

Fasten off and weave in ends.

KEY

○ ch

+ dc

⊤ tr

◄ begin row

COLOUR SEQUENCE

You can use as many colours (and scraps) as you like for this blanket, and in any order. I used the same colour for the foundation chain and rows 1 and 2, and then changed colour for each subsequent row, finishing with the same colour for the last two rows. Use either of the following methods to change colour:

• Either cut the working yarn at the end of the row and start the next row with a standing stitch (instead of a turning chain) in the new colour.

• Or change colour on the last stitch of the row by completing the final yarnover of the last stitch with the new colour, and then start the next row with ch 2 (counts as 1 tr) using the new colour.

CHART

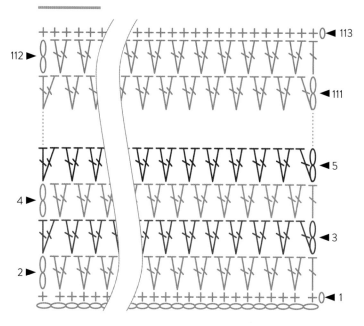

WEIMAR

What I love about this design is that it combines broad vertical stripes with narrow horizontal ones, created very simply using moss stitch (alternating chain and double crochet stitches). The geometric look is softened by the use of pastels, which are combined with bold black and white sections to give the blanket some edge. This blanket was inspired by the Bauhaus movement, which I admire greatly.

SKILL LEVEL

Easy

SIZE

Approx. 65 x 95cm (25 x 38in)

YARN

DK-weight cotton yarn in 4 colours:
- Aqua – 250m (273yd)
- Off-white – 357m (390yd)
- Beige – 179m (195yd)
- Black – 131m (143yd)

HOOK

4mm

TIPS

- This blanket is worked lengthways. If you would prefer the stripes to run across the width of the blanket, turn the photograph a quarter (90 degrees) to get an idea of what it would look like.

- If you want to upsize the pattern, be aware that you will need to make an extra-long foundation chain – the moss stitch pattern tends to 'shrink' the fabric compared to the foundation chain.

- Never heard of moss stitch before? Other names for this pattern are granite stitch and woven stitch.

PATTERN

Multiple: 2 sts, plus 1 for foundation chain.

Foundation chain: Ch 184 + 1 (or adapt to desired length of blanket).

Row 1: 1 dc in 2nd ch from hook and in each ch to end. (184 dc)

Row 2: Ch 1, skip first dc, *1 dc in next dc, ch 1, skip 1 dc; repeat from * to last dc, 1 dc in last dc.

Row 3: Ch 1, skip first dc, *1 dc in ch-1 sp, ch 1, skip 1 dc; repeat from * to beg ch, 1 dc in beg ch.

Rows 4–121: Repeat row 3.

Note: When changing colour at beginning of row, work (sl st, ch 1) in first dc, then continue as set.

Row 122: Ch 1 (turning ch), 1 dc in each dc and ch-1 sp to beg ch, 1 dc in beg ch.

Fasten off and weave in ends.

COLOUR SEQUENCE

Foundation chain: Aqua.

Rows 1–5: Aqua (5 rows).

Rows 6–8: Off-white (3 rows).

Rows 9–11: Beige (3 rows).

Rows 12–17: Alternate 1 row off-white and 1 row beige (6 rows).

Rows 18–19: Beige (2 rows).

Rows 20–29: Off-white (10 rows).

Rows 30–59: Aqua (30 rows).

Rows 60–89: Alternate 1 row off-white and 1 row black (30 rows).

Rows 90–96: Beige (7 rows).

Rows 97–105: Alternate 1 row off-white and 1 row black (8 rows).

Rows 106–112: Beige (7 rows).

Rows 113–122: Off-white (10 rows).

CHART

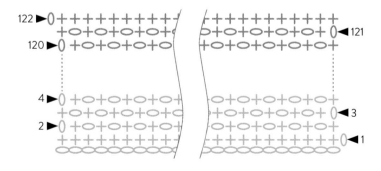

⊕ KEY

○ ch

+ dc

◀ begin row

JAIPUR

This blanket is so easy to make with only basic stitches, yet it has a
sophisticated and arty feel. The stripes are inspired by bold graphic design,
and the colour scheme by the beautiful pink city of Jaipur. The border is
an integral part of the design as it emphasises the bold pink stripes.

SKILL LEVEL

Easy

SIZE

Approx. 70 x 100cm (28 x 40in)

YARN

Aran-weight cotton yarn in 4 colours:

• Light pink – 300m (328yd)
• Dark pink – 600m (656yd)
• Off-white – 150m (164yd)
• Grey – 75m (82yd)

HOOK

5mm

TIPS

• The basic pattern is easy to remember – rows of
double crochet and rows of V-stitches (2 treble
crochet stitches with a chain in between). The
only difference between the light pink/dark pink
stripes and the off-white/grey stripes is the
number of rows worked for each stripe.

• I have started each border round with a standing
stitch and finished the round with an invisible
join, but you can begin each round with a turning
chain and finish with a slip stitch join if you
prefer (see page 124).

• If your border starts to ruffle, you can easily fix
this by switching to a smaller crochet hook – for
example, on every other row of the border.

PATTERN

Multiple: 3 sts + 2, plus 2 for foundation chain.

Foundation chain: Ch 99 + 2 + 2 (or adapt to desired width of blanket).

LIGHT PINK / DARK PINK STRIPES

Row 1: Skip first 2 ch from hook (counts as 1 tr), V-st in next ch, *skip 2 ch, V-st in next ch; repeat from * to last ch, 1 tr in last ch. (34 V-sts)

Row 2: Ch 2 (counts as 1 tr), V-st in each ch-1 sp to last st, 1 tr in last st.

Rows 3–5: Repeat row 2.

Row 6: 1 standing dc (or sl st, ch 1) in first tr, 1 dc in each tr and ch-1 sp to last st, 1 dc in last st. (104 sts)

Row 7: Ch 1 (turning ch), 1 dc in each st to end.

Rows 8–15: Repeat row 7.

Row 16: 1 standing tr (or ch 2) in first dc, skip 1 dc, *V-st in next dc, skip 2 dc; repeat from * to last 3 sts, V-st in next st, skip 1 st, 1 tr in last st. (34 V-sts)

Rows 17–75: Repeat rows 2–16 three times and then rows 2–15 once.

OFF-WHITE / GREY STRIPES

Row 76: Repeat row 16.

Row 77: Repeat row 6.

Rows 78–97: Repeat rows 76–77.

Row 98: Repeat row 16.

Rows 99–102: Repeat row 2.

Fasten off and weave in ends.

BORDER

Start in bottom right-hand corner at base of row 1 and work up right edge. Work first dc of each round as a standing dc (or sl st, ch 1).

Round 1: Work [1 dc, ch 1, 1 dc] in base of corner st, *2 dc in side of st on each of next 5 rows, skip 1 dc, 1 dc in side of st on each of next 8 rows, skip 1 dc; repeat from * to end of pink stripes. Work 2 dc in side of each tr row and 1 dc in side of each dc row to top right-hand corner. Work [1 dc, ch 1, 1 dc] in top of corner st. Work 1 dc in each tr and ch-1 sp along top of blanket to top left-hand corner. Work [1 dc, ch 1, 1 dc] in top of corner st. Work down left-hand side to match right-hand side. Work [1 dc, ch 1, 1 dc] in base of st at bottom left-hand corner. Work 1 dc in ch at base of each V-st and 2 dc in each ch-2 sp to bottom right-hand corner. Join and turn work.

Note: When working in rounds you don't usually turn your work. However, you need to do so in this pattern because otherwise the structure of the double crochet border will be different from that of the double crochet stripes in the main blanket, which would lessen the visual effect.

Rounds 2–10: Work [1 dc, ch 1, 1 dc] in each corner ch-1 sp, and 1 dc in each dc around sides. Join.

Fasten off and weave in ends.

COLOUR SEQUENCE

Foundation chain: Light pink.

Rows 1–5: Light pink (5 rows).

Rows 6–15: Dark pink (10 rows).

Rows 16–75: Alternate 5 rows light pink and 10 rows dark pink (60 rows).

Rows 76–97: Alternate 1 row off-white and 1 row grey (22 rows).

Rows 98–102: Off-white (5 rows).

Border: Dark pink (10 rounds).

BORDER CHART

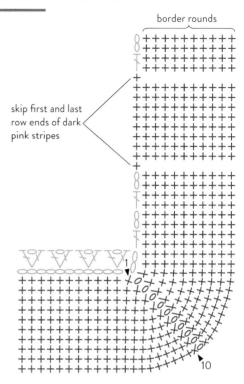

border rounds

skip first and last row ends of dark pink stripes

BLANKET CHART

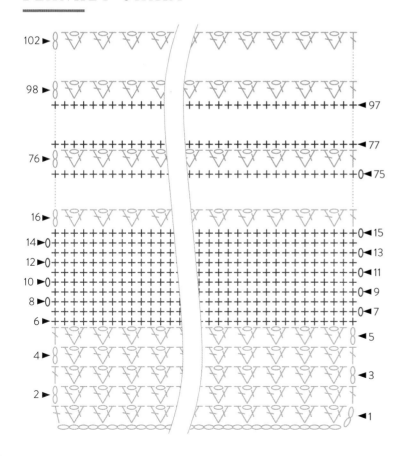

KEY

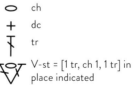

○	ch
+	dc
⊤	tr
V-st	V-st = [1 tr, ch 1, 1 tr] in place indicated
◄	begin row or round

TOKYO

I wanted to add a graphic vibe to this blanket, hence the colour blocks. Of course, this pattern would also work without them, or with stripes of colour running across the whole width of the blanket. To make the puff stitches even more distinct, I made the blanket using two strands of yarn held together throughout. This also ensures a nice, slightly slubby drape to the blanket.

SKILL LEVEL

Advanced

SIZE

Approx. 80 x 100cm (32 x 40in), excluding tassels

YARN

4ply-weight cotton yarn in 1 neutral colour and 6 accent colours:

• Beige – 1085m (1187yd)
• Dark blue – 52m (57yd)
• Green – 52m (57yd)
• Yellow – 52m (57yd)
• Dark pink – 52m (57yd)
• Light blue – 78m (85yd)
• Light pink – 78m (85yd)

HOOK

6mm

TIPS

• Vary the placement and size of the colour blocks to your own liking.
• You can either crochet over the ends of yarn as you are working, or leave them loose and weave them in afterwards.

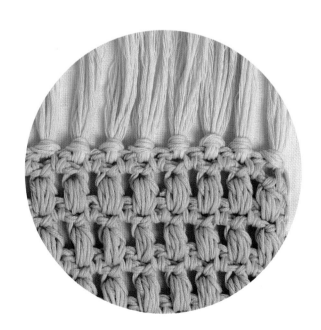

PATTERN

Multiple: 2 sts + 1, plus 1 for foundation chain.

Foundation chain: Using two strands of yarn held together throughout, ch 86 + 1 + 1 (or adapt to desired width of blanket).

Row 1: 1 dc in 2nd ch from hook, *ch 1, skip 1 ch, 1 dc in next ch; repeat from * to end. (44 dc and 43 ch-1 sps)

Row 2: Ch 2 (counts as 1 htr), skip first dc, puff st in ch-1 sp, *ch 1, skip 1 dc, puff st in next ch-1 sp; repeat from * to last dc, 1 htr in last dc. (43 puff sts)

Row 3: Ch 1 (turning ch), 1 dc in first htr, *ch 1, skip puff st, 1 dc in ch-1 sp; repeat from * to last puff st, ch 1, skip puff st, 1 dc in top of beg ch.

Rows 4–65: Repeat rows 2–3.

Note: Each colour block is composed of rows 2–4.

Fasten off and weave in ends.

TASSEL FRINGE

To soften the geometric look, I tied a fringe of simple tassels in each ch-1 sp along the top and bottom edges of the blanket.

COLOUR SEQUENCE

Work the whole blanket in the neutral colour (beige), changing to the accent colours to create colour blocks as indicated on the chart.

To change to a new colour: Work the last stitch before a colour change in the old colour, but complete the final yarnover of the stitch using the new colour. So in this pattern, if the last stitch before a new colour block is:

- Chain stitch – work the chain using the new colour.
- Double crochet – work the yarnover to complete the dc using the new colour.
- Puff stitch – work the chain that closes the puff stitch using the new colour.

Cut the old yarn at each colour change and crochet over the ends as you work or weave them in afterwards, making sure that each yarn end is hidden under stitches worked in the same colour.

Tassel fringe: Use a different accent colour for each fringe. I used light blue at the top and light pink at the bottom.

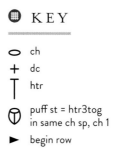

KEY

◯ ch

✛ dc

T htr

⊤ puff st = htr3tog
   in same ch sp, ch 1

▶ begin row

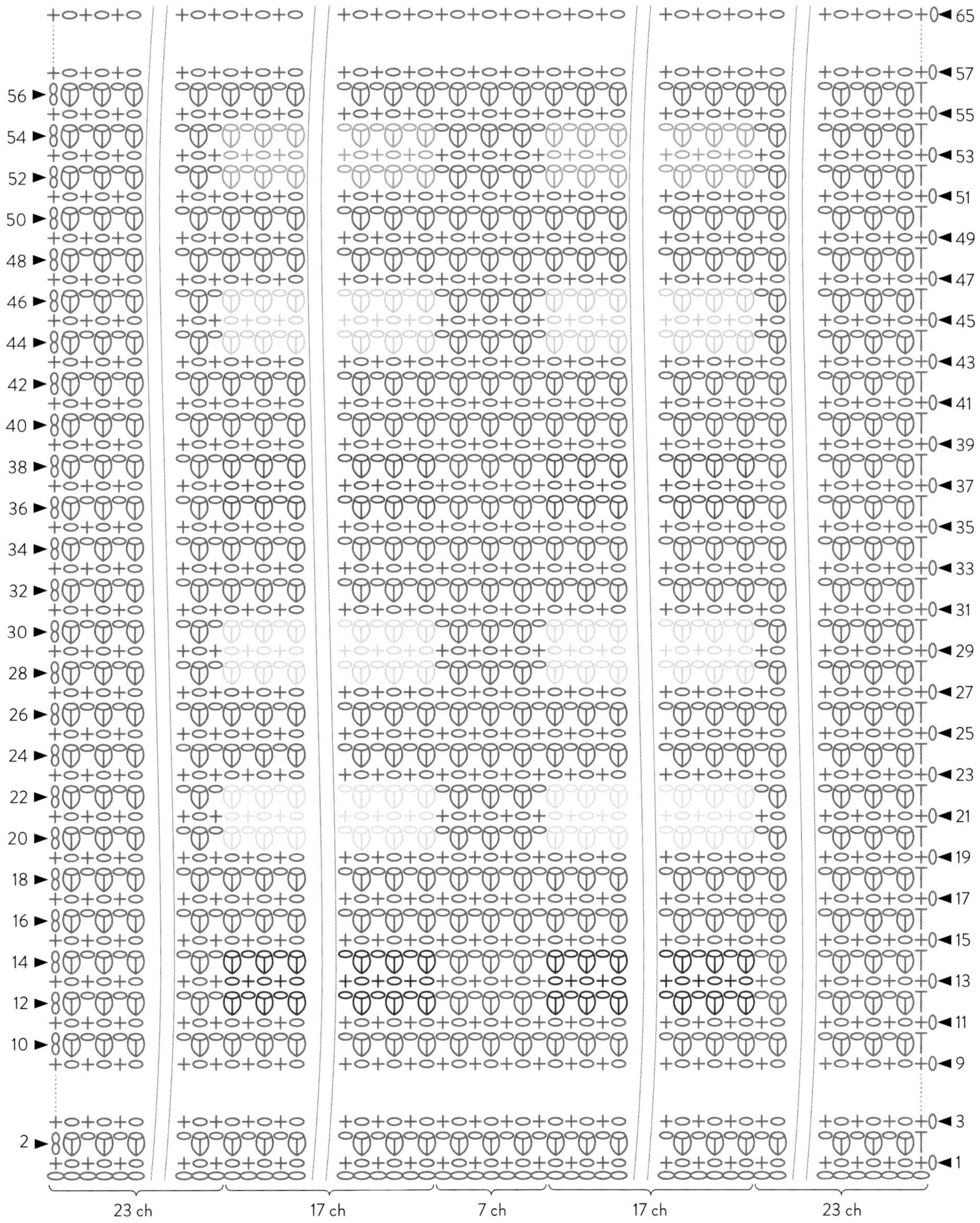

65

57

56 ► 55

54 ► 53

52 ► 51

50 ► 49

48 ► 47

46 ► 45

44 ► 43

42 ► 41

40 ► 39

38 ► 37

36 ► 35

34 ► 33

32 ► 31

30 ► 29

28 ► 27

26 ► 25

24 ► 23

22 ► 21

20 ► 19

18 ► 17

16 ► 15

14 ► 13

12 ► 11

10 ► 9

3

2 ► 1

23 ch   17 ch   7 ch   17 ch   23 ch

HAVANA

This blanket is a favourite of mine. It has a wonderful drape and is a dream to work up – no difficult stitches yet a delicate result. Once you have made the first colour stripe, the remaining stripes are just a simple repeat.

SKILL LEVEL

Intermediate

SIZE

Approx. 80 x 100cm (32 x 40in)

YARN

Aran-weight cotton yarn in 6 colours:
- Light grey – 98m (107yd)
- Off-white – 98m (107yd)
- Beige – 98m (107yd)
- Blue – 98m (107yd)
- Mustard – 98m (107yd)
- Dark grey – 98m (107yd)

HOOK

5.5mm

6mm

TIPS

For a simple variation, work the pattern so that the coloured stripes run lengthways along the blanket. All you need to do is adjust the length of the foundation chain to suit the required length of the blanket, and then work as many stripes as you wish until you achieve the desired width.

PATTERN

Multiple: 3 sts + 2, plus 2 for foundation chain.

Foundation chain: Using the larger hook, ch 90 + 2 + 2 (or adapt to desired width of blanket).

Change to the smaller hook.

Row 1: Skip first 3 ch from hook (counts as 1 tr), 1 tr in each ch to end. (92 tr)

Row 2: Ch 5 (counts as 1 tr, ch 3), skip first tr, *tr3tog over next 3 tr, ch 5; repeat from * to last 4 sts, tr3tog over next 3 sts, ch 3, 1 tr in last st.

Row 3: Ch 6 (counts as 1 dc, ch 5), [1 dc, ch 5] in each ch-5 sp to beg ch-5, skip 3 ch, 1 dc in next ch.

Row 4: Ch 3 (counts as 1 tr, ch 1), *skip 2 ch, 3 tr in next ch, skip 2 ch; repeat from * to last ch, ch 1, 1 tr in last ch.

Row 5: Ch 2 (counts as 1 tr), skip first tr, 1 tr in each tr to beg ch-3, skip 1 ch, 1 tr in next ch. (92 tr)

Row 6: 1 standing tr (or ch 2) in first tr, 1 tr in each st to end.

Rows 7–10: Repeat rows 2–5.

Rows 11–60: Repeat rows 6–10.

Fasten off and weave in ends.

⊞ KEY

○   ch
+   dc
†   tr
⋔   tr3tog
▶   begin row

COLOUR SEQUENCE

Foundation chain: Light grey.

Rows 1–5: Light grey (5 rows).

Rows 6–10: Off-white (5 rows).

Rows 11–15: Beige (5 rows).

Rows 15–20: Blue (5 rows).

Rows 21–25: Mustard (5 rows).

Rows 26–30: Dark grey (5 rows).

Rows 31–60: Repeat colour sequence of rows 1–30 (30 rows).

CHART

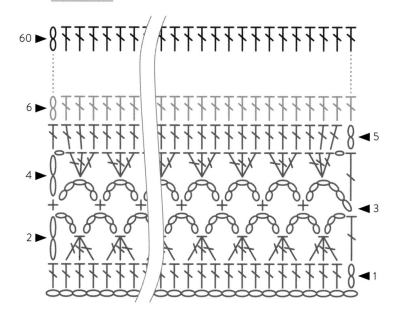

MARRAKECH

This blanket was inspired by the rich red tones of Marrakech, but it would work in any colour plan. I have used mainly scraps of yarn in various shades of red, and have chosen to contrast them with a bold black and white vertical panel in the centre to give the blanket a zesty edge.

SKILL LEVEL

Intermediate

SIZE

Approx. 70 x 100cm (28 x 40in)

YARN

DK-weight cotton yarn in 3 colourways:
- Multiple shades of red (I used 14 different shades) – 714m (780yd) in total
- Off-white – 179m (195yd)
- Black – 179m (195yd)

HOOK

4mm

4.5mm

TIPS

- You might think that there will be a lot of ends to weave in when making this blanket, but you can actually work each colour stripe with a single length of yarn by using a neat little trick to make the colour changeovers hardly visible (see page 119). This makes the blanket more durable while also reducing the number of ends considerably.

- The blanket features three vertical colour panels – black/off-white in the centre, and shades of red for the outer two panels. If you want to make a wider blanket, either add more vertical panels or stick to three but make them wider.

- For an easy variation, you could make one of the vertical panels narrower than the other two.

- This pattern is great for rugs, too, such as the Porto rug design on page 104.

PATTERN

Multiple: Any number of sts, plus 2 for foundation chain.

Foundation chain: Using the larger hook and taking care to use the correct colour sequence, ch 90 + 2 (or adapt to desired width of blanket).

Change to the smaller hook.

Row 1: Skip first 3 ch from hook (counts as 1 tr), 1 tr in each ch to end. (90 tr)

Row 2: Ch 2 (counts as 1 tr), skip first tr, 1 tr in each st to end.

Rows 3–93: Repeat row 2.

Note: When changing colour at beginning of row, work 1 standing tr (or ch 2) in first tr, then continue as set.

Fasten off and weave in ends.

COLOUR SEQUENCE

Foundation chain: Ch 30 in a shade of red (A), ch 30 in off-white (B), ch 32 in another shade of red (C).

Row 1: Work 30 tr in C, 30 tr in B, 30 tr in A.

Row 2: Work 30 tr in A, 30 tr in B, 30 tr in C.

Row 3: Work 30 tr in C, 30 tr in B, 30 tr in A.

Note: Rows 1–3 complete the first horizontal stripe. At each colour change in the middle of the blanket, work the final yarnover of the last stitch before the colour change using the new colour. See page 119 for how to make the colour changeovers neat.

Horizontal stripes: Change colours after every three rows, alternating off-white and black in the centre vertical panel, and using different shades of red in the outer vertical panels.

CHART

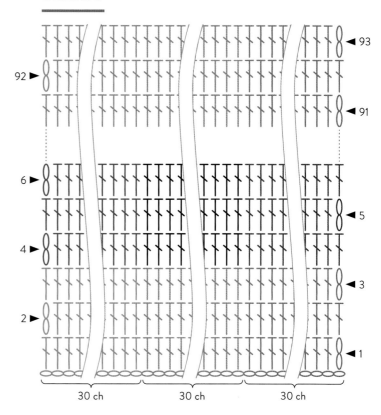

30 ch   30 ch   30 ch

⊕ KEY

◯   ch

†   tr

▶   begin row

BRUGES

Dedicated to the lace capital of Belgium, this blanket combines simple solid rows with a super-lacy flower pattern. Although the flowery parts need a bit more attention, the blanket does work up pretty quickly due to its combined lacy and solid rows. The stripes are clearly defined by the pattern, so I chose a monochrome palette to look like traditional lace.

SKILL LEVEL

Advanced

SIZE

Approx. 65 x 100cm (25 x 40in)

YARN

4ply-weight cotton yarn:
• Off-white – 697m (761yd)

HOOK

4mm

TIPS

• This pattern would work great as a curtain as well as a blanket.

• I chose a monochrome palette to echo the look of traditional lacework, but you could work the stripes in different colours if you prefer.

• I have started each border round with a standing stitch and finished the round with an invisible join, but you can begin each round with a turning chain and finish with a slip stitch join if you prefer (see page 124).

PATTERN

Multiple: 12 sts + 1, plus 2 for foundation chain.

Foundation chain: Ch 108 + 1 + 2 (or adapt to desired width of blanket).

Row 1: Skip first 3 ch from hook (counts as 1 tr), 1 tr in each ch to end. (109 tr)

Row 2: Ch 3 (counts as 1 tr, ch 1), skip first 2 tr, *1 tr in next tr, ch 1, skip 1 tr; repeat from * to last st, 1 tr in last st.

Row 3: Ch 2 (counts as 1 tr), skip first tr, 1 tr in each ch-1 sp and tr to beg ch-3, 1 tr in beg ch-3 sp, 1 tr in 2nd ch of beg ch.

FLOWER STRIPE

Row 4: Ch 7 (counts as 1 dtr, ch 4), skip first 3 tr, *[1 dc, ch 4, 2-dtr cluster] in next tr, skip 5 tr, [2-dtr cluster, ch 4, 1 dc] in next tr**, ch 9, skip 5 tr; repeat from * to last 10 sts and then from * to ** once more, ch 4, skip 2 sts, 1 dtr in last st.

Row 5: Ch 1 (turning ch), 1 dc in first dtr, ch 4, *skip cluster, [2-dtr cluster, ch 4, 1 dc, ch 4, 2-dtr cluster] in next cluster, ch 4**, 1 dc in ch-9 sp, ch 4; repeat from * to last two clusters and then from * to ** once more, 1 dc in 3rd ch of beg ch.

Row 6: Ch 6 (counts as 1 dtr, ch 2), 1 dc in first cluster, *ch 5, 1 dc in next cluster; repeat from * to last dc, ch 2, 1 dtr in last dc.

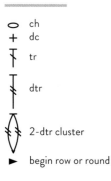

KEY

- ◯ ch
- + dc
- ⊤ tr
- dtr
- 2-dtr cluster
- ► begin row or round

BLANKET CHART

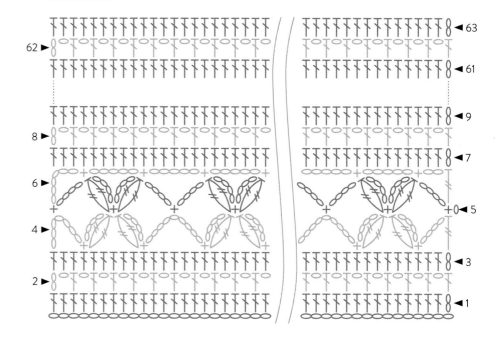

SIMPLE STRIPE

Row 7: Ch 2 (counts as 1 tr), skip first dtr, 2 tr in ch-2 sp, *1 tr in next dc, 5 tr in ch-5 sp; repeat from * to last dc, 1 tr in last dc, 2 tr in beg ch sp, 1 tr in 4th ch of beg ch.

Rows 8–9: Repeat rows 2–3.

TO COMPLETE THE BLANKET

Rows 10–63: Repeat rows 4–9.

Fasten off and weave in ends.

BORDER

Side edging: Work a row of dc along each long side of blanket, working 2 dc in the side of each tr and 3 dc in the side of each dtr (skip the side of each dc).

Now continue in rounds, starting in bottom right-hand corner at base of row 1 and working up right edge. Work first tr of each round as a standing tr (or ch 2).

Round 1: Work *[1 tr, ch 3, 1 tr] in corner st, [ch 1, skip 1 st, 1 tr in next st] to next corner st, ch 1; repeat from * 3 times. Join.

Round 2: Work [1 tr, ch 3, 1 tr] in each corner ch-3 sp, and 1 tr in each ch-1 sp and tr around sides. Join.

Round 3: Work [1 tr, ch 3, 1 tr] in each corner ch-3 sp, and along each side work [ch 1, skip 1 tr, 1 tr in next tr] to next corner ch-3 sp, ch 1. Join.

Fasten off and weave in ends.

BORDER CHART

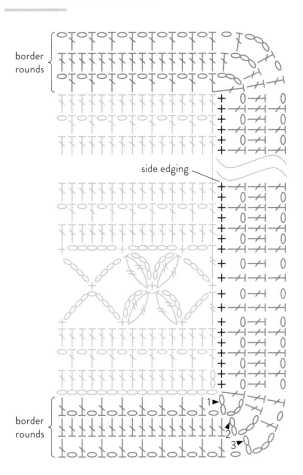

border rounds

side edging

border rounds

ST GEORGE'S

A chevron pattern is a classic for crochet blankets and I wanted to create one with a retro feel in homage to St George's, the picturesque capital of Grenada. This is an easy pattern, but with a couple of little twists. The extra-spacious gaps at the points of the chevrons create a vertical accent through the zigzag pattern, while also guaranteeing a great drape. Each colour stripe starts with back loop stitches to add a subtle layered effect.

SKILL LEVEL

Intermediate

SIZE

Approx. 85 x 100cm (34 x 40in)

YARN

DK-weight cotton yarn in 3 colours:
• Yellow – 476m (520yd)
• Aqua – 416m (455yd)
• Off-white – 179m (195yd)

HOOK

4mm

TIPS

• This pattern is essentially a repeat of the same row of treble crochet stitches, changing colours after every six and then two rows. After every colour change, remember to work the next row of treble crochet into the back loops only.

• Use this pattern to make the gorgeous Salvador bedspread on page 112.

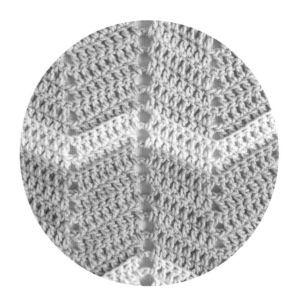

PATTERN

Multiple: 18 sts + 1, plus 2 for foundation chain.

Foundation chain: Ch 144 + 1 + 2 (or adapt to desired width of blanket).

Row 1: Skip first 2 ch from hook (counts as 1 tr), 1 tr in next ch, *1 tr in each of next 7 ch, skip 3 ch, 1 tr in each of next 7 ch**, [1 tr, ch 3, 1 tr] in next ch; repeat from * to last 18 ch and then from * to ** once more, 2 tr in last ch. (8 chevrons)

Row 2: Ch 2 (counts as 1 tr), 1 tr in first tr, *1 tr in each of next 7 tr, skip 2 tr, 1 tr in each of next 7 tr**, [1 tr, ch 3, 1 tr] in ch-3 sp; repeat from * to last 17 sts and then from * to ** once more, 2 tr in last st.

Rows 3–6: Repeat row 2.

Row 7: 1 standing BLtr (or ch 2) and 1 BLtr in first tr, *1 BLtr in each of next 7 tr, skip 2 tr, 1 BLtr in each of next 7 tr**, [1 tr, ch 3, 1 tr] in ch-3 sp; repeat from * to last 17 sts and then from * to ** once more, 2 BLtr in last st.

Rows 8–70: Repeat row 2 except for the first row after every colour change, when you should repeat row 7.

Fasten off and weave in ends.

COLOUR SEQUENCE

Foundation chain: Yellow.

Rows 1–6: Yellow (6 rows).

Rows 7–8: Off-white (2 rows).

Rows 9–14: Aqua (6 rows).

Rows 15–16: Off-white (2 rows).

Rows 17–22: Yellow (6 rows).

Rows 23–70: Repeat colour sequence of rows 7–22 three times (48 rows).

CHART

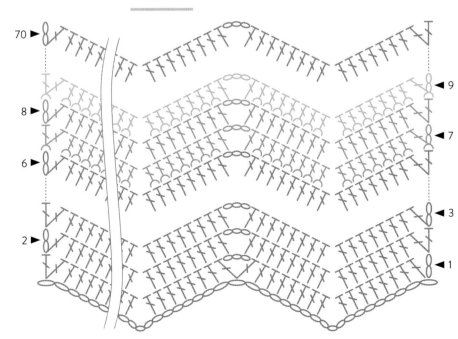

KEY

o	ch
⊤	tr
⊼	BLtr (back loop tr)
▶	begin row

HANOI

This blanket is the perfect portable project. Every stripe is crocheted separately and without the need to cut yarn, so it is easy to carry with you while travelling, even if making a full-size blanket eventually. When you have made the desired number of stripes, simply join them, add the border and voilà – a blanket that will always remind you of where and when you made it.

 SKILL LEVEL

Advanced

SIZE

Approx. 80 x100cm (32 x 40in)

YARN

Aran-weight cotton yarn in 3 colours:
- Off-white – 525m (574yd)
- Mint green – 150m (164yd)
- Pink – 113m (123yd)

HOOK

5mm

TIPS

- For my blanket I joined five stripes, but it is an easy pattern to upsize by making more and longer stripes.

- When joining the stripes, make sure you work in one direction (either from left to right, or from right to left) for the neatest result.

- The five stripes are joined together on-the-go with a lacy round of treble crochet. This results in two rows of lace where the stripes adjoin, but only one row of lace around the outside of the joined stripes. It is important to add the border to this blanket to balance the design, because it adds a second lacy row around the outside of the blanket to mirror the double rows of lace between the stripes.

- I have started each of the edging/joining/ border rounds with a standing stitch and finished the round with an invisible join, but you can begin each round with a turning chain and finish with a slip stitch join if you prefer (see page 124).

PATTERN

Foundation chain: Ch 18.

Row 1: Skip first 3 ch from hook (counts as 1 tr), 1 tr in each ch to end. (16 tr)

Row 2: Ch 2 (counts as 1 tr throughout), skip first tr, 1 tr in each of next 6 tr, ch 3, skip 2 tr, 1 tr in each of last 7 sts.

Row 3: Ch 2, skip first tr, 1 tr in each of next 3 tr, ch 4, skip 3 tr, 1 dc in ch-3 sp, ch 4, skip 3 tr, 1 tr in each of last 4 sts.

Row 4: Ch 2, skip first tr, 1 tr in next tr, [ch 4, 1 dc in next ch-4 sp] twice, ch 4, 1 tr in each of last 2 sts.

Row 5: Ch 2, skip first tr, 1 tr in next tr, 2 tr in ch-4 sp, ch 4, 1 dc in next ch-4 sp, ch 4, 2 tr in next ch-4 sp, 1 tr in each of last 2 sts.

Row 6: Ch 2, skip first tr, 1 tr in each of next 3 tr, 3 tr in ch-4 sp, ch 2, 3 tr in next ch-4 sp, 1 tr in each of last 4 sts.

Row 7: Ch 2, skip first tr, 1 tr in each of next 6 tr, 2 tr in ch-2 sp, 1 tr in each of last 7 sts.

Rows 8–61: Repeat rows 2–7.

Fasten off and weave in ends.

EDGING EACH STRIPE

This first round of edging ensures a neat finish, plus it will be the basis for joining the stripes later.

Round 1: Starting in top-left corner, work 1 standing dc (or sl st, ch 1) in top of corner st, ch 3, 1 dc in side of same st (corner made), [ch 2, 1 dc] in side of each st to bottom-left corner, ch 3, skip first foundation ch, [1 dc in next ch, ch 2, skip 1 ch] seven times along bottom edge, 1 dc in next ch, ch 3, 1 dc in side of first st of row 1, [ch 2, 1 dc] in side of each st to top-right corner, ch 3, skip top of corner st, [1 dc in top of next tr, ch 2, skip 1 tr] seven times along top edge. Join.

Fasten off and weave in ends.

Make and edge five stripes in total.

JOINING THE STRIPES

Work a second round of edging around the stripe that will be on the left-hand side of the blanket as follows:

Round 2: Starting in first dc at top-left corner, work 1 standing tr (or ch 2) in corner dc, ch 5, 1 tr in next corner dc, *[ch 1, 1 tr] in each dc to next corner, ch 5, [1 tr in next dc, ch 1] seven times**, 1 tr in next dc, ch 5, 1 tr in next corner dc; repeat from * to **. Join.

Fasten off and weave in ends.

Now work round 2 around the next stripe, but join it to the first stripe at the same time by substituting each ch-1 along the adjoining side with a sl st into the adjacent ch-1 sp of the first stripe. At the adjoining corners, substitute the middle ch of the corner ch-5 with a sl st into the corner ch-5 sp of the first stripe.

Join the remaining three stripes in the same way.

BORDER

Round 3: Starting in first tr at top-left corner, work 1 standing tr (or ch 2) in corner tr, *ch 3, [1 tr, ch 3, 1 tr] in 3rd ch of corner ch-5, ch 3, 1 tr in next tr, [ch 2, 1 tr] in each tr to next corner ch-5; repeat from * to start of round, working 1 dtr into the sl st joins between stripes to ensure a straight border. Join.

Round 4: Work as round 3 but start with a standing dc (or sl st, ch 1) and substitute 1 dc in place of each tr and dtr around. Join.

Fasten off and weave in ends.

COLOUR SEQUENCE

Stripes: 3 off-white, 1 mint green, 1 pink.

Edging and joining the stripes: Use the same colour as the stripe you are working.

Border: Off-white (round 1) and mint green (round 2).

CHART

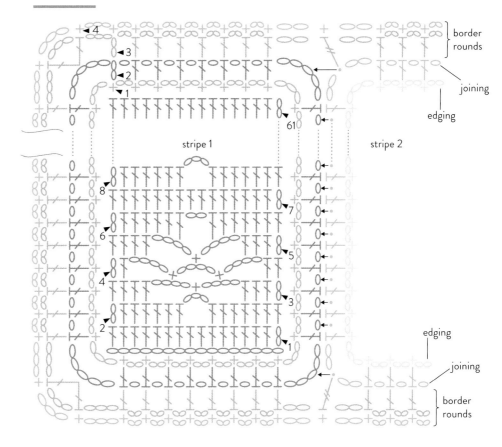

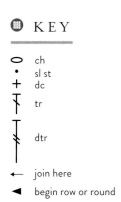

KEY

- ⭕ ch
- • sl st
- ✛ dc
- ⭾ tr
- ⭾ dtr
- ← join here
- ◄ begin row or round

SEOUL

Simple yet refined, this blanket is the result of combining the sober double crochet stitch with the lesser-used triple treble stitch. The combination of a short and a super-long stitch creates an interesting texture, wonderful drape and is a guarantee for enjoyable crochet time. The pattern would also look great worked in a chunky yarn to make a comfortable throw.

SKILL LEVEL

Intermediate

SIZE

Approx. 65 x 95cm (25 x 38in)

YARN

DK-weight cotton blend yarn in as many colours as you wish:

• Each stripe – 50m (55yd)

HOOK

4mm

TIPS

• Looking for a more pronounced contrast between short and elevated stitches? Substitute the triple treble (trtr) with a quadruple treble (quadtr: yarnover x 4), a quintuple treble (quintr: yarnover x 5) or an even longer stitch.

• I have used a ch-5 here to begin each row of triple trebles. Depending on your tension/crochet style/yarn, you may prefer to use a ch-6 if you feel that you need a longer chain. You could use a standing stitch instead, but it is a bit fiddly for a long stitch.

• For an interesting colour effect, try using a contrasting colour for each middle row of double crochet throughout the blanket.

PATTERN

Multiple: Any number of sts, plus 1 for foundation chain.

Foundation chain: Ch 88 + 1 (or adapt to desired width of blanket).

Row 1: 1 dc in 2nd ch from hook and in each ch to end. (88 dc)

Row 2: Ch 1 (turning ch), 1 dc in each st to end.

Row 3: Repeat row 2.

Row 4: Ch 5 (counts as 1 trtr), skip first dc, 1 trtr in each dc to end. (88 trtr)

Row 5: 1 standing dc (or sl st, ch 1) in first trtr, 1 dc in each st to end.

Rows 6–60: Repeat rows 2–5 thirteen times and then rows 2–4 once.

Row 61: Ch 1 (turning ch), 1 dc in each trtr to end. Fasten off and weave in ends.

COLOUR SEQUENCE

4-row stripes: Change colour after every four rows, working each stripe in any colour you like and in any sequence of colours. Simply remember to change colour after every row of triple treble stitches, except after the last row of triple trebles.

To finish: Work the final row of double crochet stitches in the same colour as the last row of triple trebles. This final row of double crochet gives the upper edge of the blanket some extra firmness to help keep it in shape.

CHART

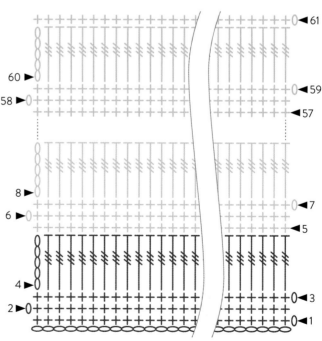

● KEY

○	ch
+	dc
⫢	trtr
►	begin row

ODESSA

I love solid, slightly textured stitches because they catch the light in such a subtle way. I found it hard to choose which stitch patterns to include in this book, so I made this blanket using seven of my favourites, changing stitch pattern for each colour stripe. You can use the same sequence of stitch patterns as I have, or just pick the stitches you like best for your blanket.

SKILL LEVEL

Advanced

SIZE

Approx. 90 x 105cm (35 x 41in)

YARN

4ply-weight cotton yarn in
as many colours as you wish:

• Each stripe – 186m (203yd)

HOOK

3.5mm

TIPS

• Some of the stitch patterns used in this blanket have several names. For example, urchin stitch is also known as spider stitch, while granite stitch is also known as moss or woven stitch.

• Note that each stripe consists of a different number of rows. This is to make sure that all the stripes are the same depth, despite being worked in different stitch patterns.

PATTERN

Multiple: 2 sts + 1, plus 1 for foundation chain.

Foundation chain: Ch 90 + 1 + 1 (or adapt to desired width of blanket).

STRIPE 1 – LEMON PEEL STITCH (16 ROWS)
Row 1: 1 tr in 2nd ch from hook (first ch counts as 1 dc), *1 dc in next ch, 1 tr in next ch; repeat from * to end.

Rows 2–16: Ch 1 (counts as 1 dc), skip first tr, *1 tr in next dc, 1 dc in next tr; repeat from * to last st, 1 tr in last st.

STRIPE 2 – GRIT STITCH (16 ROWS)
Row 17: 1 standing dc (or sl st, ch 1) and 1 tr in first tr, [1 dc, 1 tr] in each tr to last tr, 1 dc in last tr.

Rows 18–32: Ch 1 (counts as 1 dc), 1 tr in first dc, [1 dc, 1 tr] in each dc to last st, 1 dc in last st.

STRIPE 3 – URCHIN / SPIDER STITCH (18 ROWS)
Row 33: 1 standing htr (or ch 2) in first dc, [1 dc, ch 2, 1 dc] in each tr to last st, 1 htr in last st.

Rows 34–50: Ch 2 (counts as 1 htr), [1 dc, ch 2, 1 dc] in each ch-2 sp to last st, 1 htr in last st.

STRIPE 4 – TRINITY STITCH (20 ROWS)
Row 51: 1 standing dc (or sl st, ch 1) in first htr, *ch 1, dc3tog worked over next [1 dc, ch-2 sp, 1 dc]; repeat from * to last st, ch 1, 1 dc in last st.

Rows 52–70: Ch 1 (turning ch), 1 dc in first dc, *ch 1, dc3tog over [ch-1 sp, dc3tog, ch-1 sp]; working first leg of each dc3tog in same ch-1 sp as last leg of previous dc3tog, repeat from * to last st, ch 1, 1 dc in last st.

STRIPE 5 – EVEN MOSS STITCH (24 ROWS)
Row 71: 1 standing htr (or ch 2) in first dc, sl st in first dc3tog, *1 htr in next ch-1 sp, sl st in next dc3tog; repeat from * to last st, 1 htr in last st.

Row 72: Sl st in first htr, *1 htr in next sl st, sl st in next htr; repeat from * to end.

Row 73: Ch 2 (counts as 1 htr), skip first sl st, *sl st in next htr, 1 htr in next sl st; repeat from * to end.

Rows 74–94: Repeat rows 72–73, ending with a row 72.

STRIPE 6 – MOSS / GRANITE / WOVEN STITCH (20 ROWS)
Row 95: (Sl st, ch 1) in first sl st, 1 dc in first htr, [ch 1, 1 dc] in each htr to end, 1 dc in last sl st.

Row 96: Ch 1, [ch 1, 1 dc] in each ch-1 sp to last dc, ch 1, skip last dc, 1 dc in beg ch.

Row 97: Ch 1, [1 dc, ch 1] in each ch-1 sp to beg ch sp, 1 dc in beg ch sp, 1 dc in first ch of beg ch.

Rows 98–114: Repeat rows 96–97, ending with a row 96.

STRIPE 7 – BACK LOOP DOUBLE CROCHET (20 ROWS)
Row 115: 1 standing dc (or sl st, ch 1) in first dc, 1 dc in each ch sp and dc to end, 1 dc in last ch.

Rows 116–136: Ch 1 (turning ch), 1 BLdc in each dc to end.

STRIPES 8, 9, AND 10
Row 137: 1 standing dc (or sl st, ch 1) and 1 tr in first dc, *1 dc in next dc, 1 tr in next dc; repeat from * to end.

Rows 138–186: Repeat rows 2–16 of stripe 1, then all rows of stripes 2 and 3.

Fasten off and weave in ends.

COLOUR SEQUENCE

Work each stripe in a different colour or repeat colours as desired, either in a set sequence or at random. In the sample shown, I have used the same colour for stripes 3 and 10, and a different colour for all the others.

KEY

○	ch
•	sl st
+	dc
大	BLdc (back loop dc)
T	htr
Ŧ	tr
木	dc3tog
▶	begin row

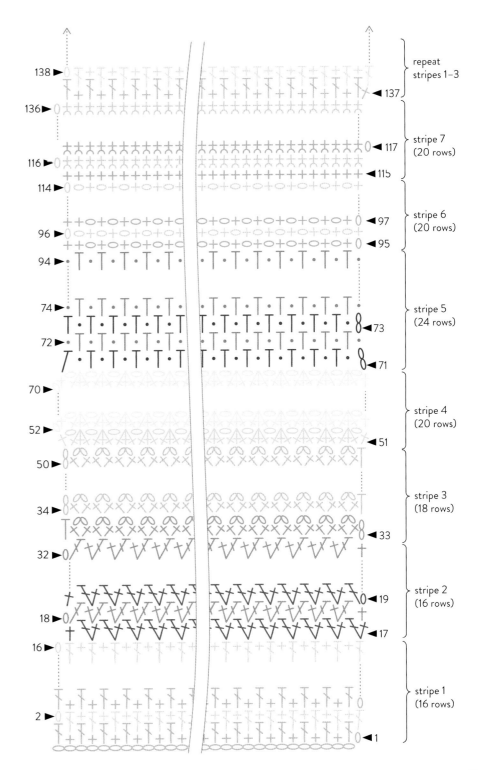

repeat stripes 1–3

stripe 7 (20 rows)

stripe 6 (20 rows)

stripe 5 (24 rows)

stripe 4 (20 rows)

stripe 3 (18 rows)

stripe 2 (16 rows)

stripe 1 (16 rows)

LISBON

I have named this blanket after one of my favourite cities. Like Lisbon, the blanket is pastel-coloured and has a distinct 1950s feel. But if you are looking for something bolder, this geometric pattern would look striking in black and white. It is a straightforward blanket to make, with the rows seeming to work themselves once you get into the rhythm of the pattern. Alternating short and long stitches creates a beautifully tactile blanket.

SKILL LEVEL

Intermediate

SIZE

Approx. 75 x 110cm (30 x 43in)

YARN

Aran-weight cotton yarn in 2 colours:
• Mint green – 637m (697yd)
• Off-white – 563m (615yd)

HOOK

5.5mm

6mm

TIPS

• This pattern is perfect for downsizing to make small projects such as the Chiang Mai potholder and dish towel on page 106.

• I have started each border round with a standing stitch and finished the round with an invisible join, but you can begin each round with a turning chain and finish with a slip stitch join if you prefer (see page 124).

PATTERN

Multiple: 2 sts + 1, plus 1 for foundation chain.

Foundation chain: Using the larger hook,
ch 84 + 1 + 1 (or adapt to desired width of blanket).

Change to the smaller hook.

Row 1: Skip first ch from hook (counts as 1 dc),
1 tr in next ch, skip 1 ch, *[1 dc, 1 tr] in next ch,
skip 1 ch; repeat from * to last ch, 1 dc in last ch.
(42 [1 dc, 1 tr] groups)

Row 2: 1 standing dc (or sl st, ch 1) and 1 tr in first dc,
*skip 1 tr, [1 dc, 1 tr] in next dc; repeat from * to last
2 sts, skip 1 st, 1 dc in last st.

Rows 3–118: Repeat row 2.

Fasten off and weave in ends.

BORDER

Start in top-right corner st and work first st of each
round as a standing dc (or sl st, ch 1).

Round 1: Work [1 dc, ch 3, 1 dc] in corner st, [ch 2, 1 dc]
in each dc along top edge to next corner, [ch 3, 1 dc]
in same corner st, [ch 2, skip 1 row, 1 dc in side of
next row] down left side of blanket to next corner
(note that you are working 1 dc into the side of each
even-numbered row worked in off-white yarn), ch 2,
[1 dc, ch 3, 1 dc] in bottom-left corner st, [ch 2, 1 dc]
in each tr of row 1 along bottom edge to next corner,
ch 2, [1 dc, ch 3, 1 dc] in bottom-right corner st;
work right side of blanket to match left side. Join.

Round 2: Work 3 dc in each corner ch-3 sp, and
2 dc in each ch-2 sp around sides. Join.

Fasten off and weave in ends.

COLOUR SEQUENCE

Foundation chain: Mint green.

Row 1: Mint green (1 row).

Row 2: Off-white (1 row).

Rows 3–118: Alternate 1 row mint green
and 1 row off-white (116 rows).

Border: Mint green (2 rounds).

BLANKET CHART

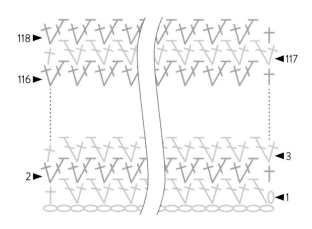

● KEY

○ ch
+ dc
Ŧ tr
◀ begin row or round

BORDER CHART

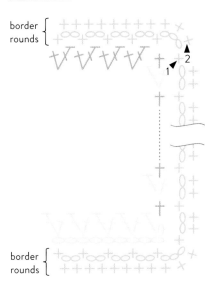

ISTANBUL

The elegant chevron-shaped chains look like little laurels and ensure a wonderful texture. The reverse of this blanket looks completely different from the front, but has an equally beautiful structure. The colour pattern is intriguing too, with every new colour announcing itself by one modest row set within the previous colour.

SKILL LEVEL

Advanced

SIZE

Approx. 65 x 95cm (25 x 38in)

YARN

Aran-weight cotton yarn in 5 colours:
- Dark blue – 150m (164yd)
- Beige – 150m (164yd)
- Green – 75m (82yd)
- Pink – 300m (328yd)
- Light blue – 75m (82yd)

HOOK

5.5mm

TIPS

- Each main stripe consists of 14 rows, using a contrast colour for the 12th row. The contrast colour then becomes the main colour for the next stripe.

- The chevrons are formed by working a length of chain that is slip stitched at the centre into a chain space two rows below. So the chains on row 4 are slip stitched into chain spaces on row 2, those on row 6 are slip stitched into row 4 and so on.

- Treble crochet stitches are worked on each wrong-side row after a chevron chain. These are also worked into stitches two rows below, so the trebles on row 5 are worked into row 3, those on row 7 and worked into row 5 and so on. Take care to work the trebles in front of the chevron chains from the previous row, so that the chevrons will lie on the right side of the blanket.

- I have started each border round with a standing stitch and finished the round with an invisible join, but you can begin each round with a turning chain and finish with a slip stitch join if you prefer (see page 124).

PATTERN

Multiple: 14 sts + 5, plus 1 for foundation chain.

Foundation chain: Ch 84 + 5 + 1 (or adapt to desired width of blanket).

Row 1 (WS): 1 dc in 2nd ch from hook and in each ch to end. (89 dc)

Row 2: Ch 1 (turning ch throughout), 1 dc in first dc, *ch 1, skip 1 dc, 1 dc in next dc; repeat from * to end.

Row 3: Ch 1, 1 dc in first dc, *ch 1, skip 1 ch, 1 dc in next dc; repeat from * to end.

Row 4: Ch 1, 1 dc in first dc, [ch 1, skip 1 ch, 1 dc in next dc] twice, *ch 5, skip [1 ch, 1 st, 1 ch, 1 st], sl st in next ch-1 sp two rows below, ch 5, skip [1 st, 1 ch, 1 st, 1 ch], 1 dc in next dc, [ch 1, skip 1 ch, 1 dc in next dc] twice; repeat from * to end. (6 chevron chains)

Row 5: Ch 1, 1 dc in first dc, [ch 1, skip 1 ch, 1 dc in next dc] twice, *ch 1, [working in front of ch-5 from previous row: 1 tr in next st two rows below, ch 1, skip 1 ch] four times, 1 dc in next dc, [ch 1, skip 1 ch, 1 dc in next dc] twice; repeat from * to end.

Rows 6–100: Repeat rows 4–5, ending with a row 4.

Note: When changing colour at beginning of row, work 1 standing dc (or sl st, ch 1) in first dc, then continue as set. Work last st of next row into standing dc (or ch-1).

Row 101: Ch 1, 1 dc in first dc, [ch 1, skip 1 ch, 1 dc in next dc] twice, *ch 1, [working in front of ch-5 from previous row: 1 dc in next tr two rows below, ch 1, skip 1 ch] four times, 1 dc in next dc, [ch 1, skip 1 ch, 1 dc in next dc] twice; repeat from * to end.

Row 102: Ch 1, 1 dc in each dc and ch sp to end.

Fasten off and weave in ends.

BORDER

Start in any corner dc and work first st of each round as a standing dc (or sl st, ch 1).

Round 1: Work [1 dc, ch 1, 1 dc] in corner dc (corner made), *ch 1, skip 1 dc, 1 dc in next dc; repeat from * to next corner, then work around remainder of blanket to match. Join and turn work.

Note: When working in rounds you don't usually turn your work. However, you need to do so in this pattern because otherwise the structure of the double crochet and chain stitch border will be different from that in the main blanket, which would lessen the visual effect.

Round 2: At each corner work 1 dc in first corner dc, ch 3, 1 dc in next corner dc. Work around each side to match round 1, working 1 dc into each dc, and ch 1 above each ch. Join and turn work.

Rounds 3–9: Repeat round 2, increasing the number of chains at each corner by 1 on every new round. So round 9 will have 10 ch at each corner (or adjust to your tension and/or preference for a wider corner).

Fasten off and weave in ends.

COLOUR SEQUENCE

Foundation chain: Main colour (dark blue).

Rows 1–2: Main colour (dark blue).

Stripe 1 (rows 3–16): 11 rows main colour (dark blue: rows 2–13), 1 row contrast colour (beige: row 14), 2 rows main colour (dark blue: rows 15–16).

Remaining stripes (rows 17–100): Work each 14-row stripe in any colour you like, using the contrast colour from the previous stripe as the main colour for each new stripe. In the sample shown, the main colours for the remaining six stripes are: beige, green, pink, light blue, dark blue, beige.

Rows 101–102: Final main colour (beige).

Border: Main colour of middle stripe (pink).

KEY

- ⬭ ch
- • sl st
- ✛ dc
- ⊤ tr
- ◀ begin row or round

BORDER CHART

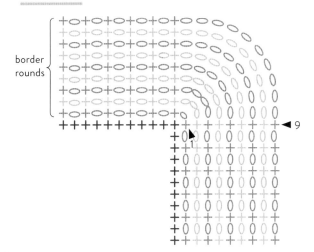

border rounds

BLANKET CHART

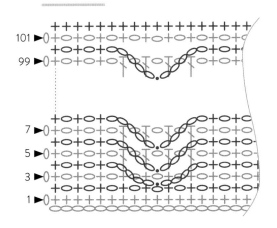
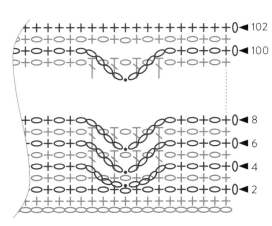

NAIROBI

Diagonal stripes, worked from one corner to the diagonally opposite corner, make a welcome variation on horizontal and vertical stripes.
I wanted to create a blanket with an airy feel, and the easy double treble crochet stitches work up quickly in this blanket. In the first half of the pattern you will be increasing to form a triangle shape, and in the second half decreasing to form a matching triangle, resulting in a square blanket.

SKILL LEVEL

Easy

SIZE

Approx. 100 x 100cm (40 x 40in)

YARN

4ply-weight cotton yarn in 4 colours:

• Light pink – 310m (339yd)

• Mid-pink – 310m (339yd)

• Dusky pink – 310m (339yd)

• Pale peach – 310m (339yd)

HOOK

4mm

TIPS

• I have changed colours after every five rows using a random sequence of four colours, but you could use more or fewer colours if you wish. You can also vary the depth of the stripes by changing colours after a different number of rows.

• Although this pattern starts with a foundation ring, you are working the blanket in rows, so remember to turn the work at the end of each row.

• There are 79 rows in the blanket. You increase the number of stitches on each row for the first 40 rows, with row 40 being the widest row in the blanket, and then decrease on the remaining 39 rows. If you wish to make a bigger blanket, simply continue increasing until you reach the desired dimensions before decreasing. To make a smaller blanket, work fewer than 40 rows until you reach the desired size and then decrease.

PATTERN

Foundation ring: Ch 4 and join with sl st to form a ring.

Row 1: Ch 6 (counts as 1 dtr, ch 2 on each row to last row), [4 dtr, ch 2, 1 dtr] in ring.

Row 2: Ch 6, [4 dtr, ch 2] in first ch sp, [4 dtr, ch 2, 1 dtr] in next ch sp.

Rows 3–40: Ch 6, [4 dtr, ch 2] in each ch sp to last ch sp, [4 dtr, ch 2, 1 dtr] in last ch sp.

You will now start decreasing.

Rows 41–78: Ch 6, skip first ch sp, [4 dtr, ch 2] in each ch sp to last ch sp, 1 dtr in last ch sp.

Row 79: Ch 6, skip first ch sp, dtr4tog in next ch sp, ch 6, skip 4 tr and 2 ch, sl st in next ch.

Fasten off and weave in ends.

CHART

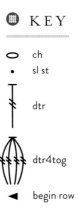

COLOUR SEQUENCE

Foundation ring: Pale peach.

Rows 1–5: Pale peach (5 rows).

Rows 6–10: Dusky pink (5 rows).

Rows 11–15: Light pink (5 rows).

Rows 16–20: Pale peach (5 rows).

Rows 21–25: Mid-pink (5 rows).

Rows 26–30: Light pink (5 rows).

Rows 31–35: Dusky pink (5 rows).

Rows 36–40: Mid-pink (5 rows).

Rows 41–45: Pale peach (5 rows).

Rows 46–50: Light pink (5 rows).

Rows 51–55: Dusky pink (5 rows).

Rows 56–60: Mid-pink (5 rows).

Rows 61–65: Light pink (5 rows).

Rows 66–70: Pale peach (5 rows).

Rows 71–75: Mid-pink (5 rows).

Rows 76–79: Light pink (4 rows).

⊞ KEY

⬭	ch
•	sl st
⑂	dtr
🖌	dtr4tog
◄	begin row

CASABLANCA

I am a huge admirer of the colourful boucherouite 'rag rugs' from Morocco. The ragged look and geometric patterns are stunning, so I decided to create a blanket with the same colourful, scrappy look – and I am delighted with the result. Also, you hardly have to weave in any ends because you use most of them to assemble the blanket.

 SKILL LEVEL

Intermediate

SIZE

Approx. 90 x 110cm (35 x 43in)

YARN

Aran-weight cotton yarn in as many colours as you wish:

• Total quantity – 900m (984yd)

HOOK

6mm

TIPS

• This pattern is a guideline for creating your own 'organised mess' blanket. The chart for the main centre panel shows examples of how to combine the different stitch variations, but it is up to you exactly where you position them and how many of each variation you use – you can mix and match them as you wish.

• To produce a boucherouite effect, use as many bright and pastel colours as you have, apply a generous amount of off-white and add some black and other darker hues for contrast.

• To create the slightly shabby look of a rag rug, it is important to upsize your hook considerably from the size you would normally use for Aran-weight yarn. I usually work this yarn with a 5mm hook, but upsized to a 6mm for this blanket.

• Why not make a matching boucherouite cushion to go with the blanket, using the Shiraz cushion design on page 108?

PATTERN

Note: The centre panel and side border panels are each worked separately. Start and end each new colour with a generous tail of yarn. You will need these to tie the panels together – only the outer ends will need to be woven in. After the centre and side panels have been assembled, the top and bottom border panels are crocheted directly on to the top and bottom edges to complete the blanket.

CENTRE PANEL

Multiple: Any number of sts, plus 2 for foundation chain.

Foundation chain: Ch 60 + 2 (or adapt to desired width of blanket).

Row 1: Skip first 3 ch from hook (counts as 1 htr), 1 htr in each ch to end. (60 htr)

Row 2: 1 standing htr (or ch 2) in first htr, 1 htr in each st to end.

Rows 3–65: Repeat row 2, but vary as follows to create a rag rug effect:

- Substitute a group of htr from time to time with either dc or tr.
- Play with texture by working these groups of dc and tr in either back loops only or front loops only.
- To make sure the blanket retains straight edges and does not become wonky, if you have worked a group of tr on one row, work dc on top of them in the next row. Likewise, if you have worked a group of dc on one row, work tr on top of them in the next row. On the following row you can work htr as usual.

Fasten off but do not weave in ends.

SIDE BORDER PANELS

Multiple: Any number of sts, plus 2 for foundation chain.

Foundation chain: Ch 14 + 2.

Row 1: Skip first 3 ch from hook (counts as 1 tr), 1 tr in each ch to end. (14 tr)

Row 2: Ch 2 (counts as 1 tr), skip first tr, 1 tr in each st to end.

Rows 3–32: Repeat row 2.

Note: When changing colour at beginning of row, work 1 standing tr (or ch 2) in first tr, then continue as set.

Fasten off but do not weave in ends.

ASSEMBLING CENTRE AND SIDE PANELS

This could not be easier! Lay the three panels out in front of you and weave all ends on the side panels towards the inner edges that will be joined. Now gently tie the side panels to the centre panel, using the ends. There should be sufficient yarn for a sturdy join, but you can use extra yarn if necessary. Make sure all the ends are tied on the same side of the blanket (front or reverse, depending on how scrappy you want the blanket to look). Trim them if necessary, but don't cut them off completely – they are part of the design.

TOP AND BOTTOM BORDER PANELS

Join yarn to top-right corner st of blanket.

Row 1: Ch 2 (counts as 1 tr), skip first st, 1 tr in each st to end.

Rows 2–6: Repeat row 1.

Fasten off and weave in ends.

Repeat along bottom edge of blanket.

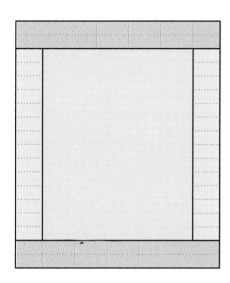

COLOUR SEQUENCE

Centre panel: Change colour for every row.

Side border panels: Change colour after every 3 rows. Occasionally use two different shades of a colour in the same 3-row stripe – ideal if you are working with scraps, plus it adds to the boucherouite look.

Top and bottom border panels: Use 5 colours per row, creating colour blocks of any width you like using the same colour-changing technique as the Marrakech blanket (see page 119).

CHARTS

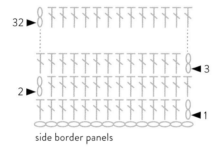

side border panels

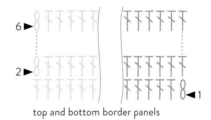

top and bottom border panels

KEY

0	ch
+	dc
‡	FLdc (front loop dc)
⊼	BLdc (back loop dc)
T	htr
Ŧ	tr
◄	begin row

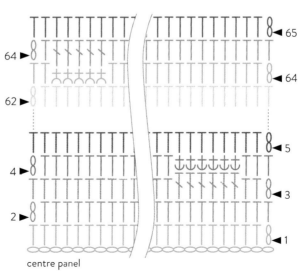

centre panel

OSLO

Some textiles have such lovely surfaces that you just have to touch them. The astrakhan and double loop stitches used in this blanket definitely qualify as irresistibly tactile. Browse forwards to the project chapter to see how you can turn this pattern into the beautiful Fez wall hanging (page 110).

SKILL LEVEL

Advanced

SIZE

Approx. 65 x 100cm (25 x 40in)

YARN

Aran-weight cotton yarn in 1 neutral colour and 5 accent colours:

- Grey – 375m (410yd)
- Dusky pink (top and bottom stripes) – 150m (164yd)
- 4 more shades of pink/peach – 75m (82yd) each

HOOK

5.5mm

TIPS

- It is advisable to upsize your hook slightly for this pattern. I usually work Aran-weight yarn with a 5mm hook, but upsized to a 5.5mm for this blanket.

- Double loop stitch is really just a double crochet stitch but with little tweaks to make the loops. The important thing is that it must be worked with the wrong side of the fabric facing you, because the loops appear on the other (right) side, so keep this in mind if you change the number of rows in your blanket.

- The pattern has two consecutive rows of double loop stitch, so you have to cut and rejoin the yarn to start the second row at the same side as the first one. This way the loops from both rows will appear on the right side of the fabric, creating a dense loop structure.

- Although the pattern starts with odd-numbered rows for the right side and even-numbered rows for the wrong side, this varies throughout the pattern because of working the two consecutive rows of double loop stitch from the wrong side. Just remember that the wrong side of the blanket should face you for all double loop stitches, and the right side should face you for all asktrakhan stitches.

- All stitches worked through the front loop should be worked in the loop nearest to you, whether the right side or wrong side of the blanket is facing you.

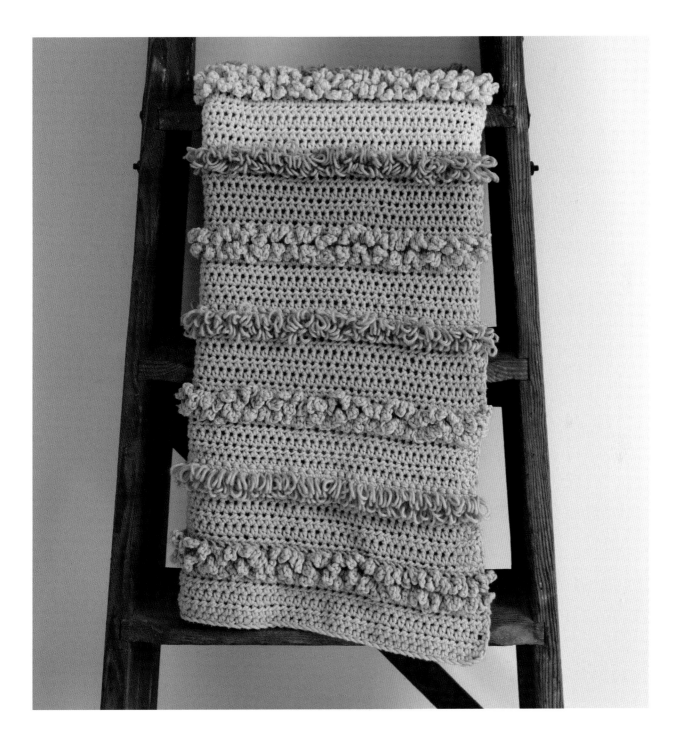

KEY

○ ch

• sl st

T htr

↓ FLhtr (front loop htr)

∪ astrakhan stitch = ch 6,
sl st in front loop of next st

⊎ double loop stitch (see Special stitch)

⌇ work into sts two rows below

◄ begin row

SPECIAL STITCH

Double loop stitch = Wrap yarn over index finger of
left hand (if you are right-handed) twice. Insert hook
in next stitch and wrap hook around working yarn in
opposite direction to normal (anticlockwise). Insert
hook behind two strands of yarn on your finger and pull
them from behind your finger; then pull them and the
working yarn (three loops in total) through the stitch.
You now have four loops on the hook. Continue as
a regular dc: yo and pull through all loops on hook.
Let the double loop of yarn slide off your index finger.

CHART

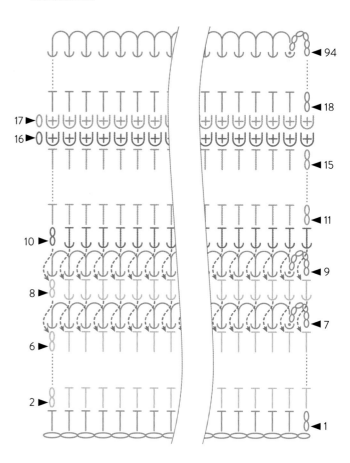

PATTERN

Multiple: Any number of sts, plus 2 for foundation chain.

Foundation chain: Ch 75 + 2 (or adapt to desired width of blanket).

ASTRAKHAN STRIPE

Row 1: Skip first 3 ch from hook (counts as 1 htr), 1 htr in each ch to end. (75 htr)

Row 2: Ch 2 (counts as 1 htr), skip first htr, 1 htr in each st to end.

Rows 3–6: Repeat row 2.

Row 7 (RS) (astrakhan st): Skip first htr, *ch 6, sl st in front loop of next st; repeat from * to end.

Row 8: Working into front (unworked) loops of each htr two rows below, ch 2 (counts as 1 FLhtr), skip first st, *1 FLhtr in each st to end.

Row 9 (RS) (astrakhan st): Repeat row 7.

DOUBLE LOOP STRIPE

Row 10: Working into front (unworked) loops of each htr two rows below, 1 standing FLhtr (or ch 2) in first st, *1 FLhtr in each st to end.

Rows 11–15: Repeat row 2.

Row 16 (WS) (double loop st): Ch 1 (turning ch), 1 double loop st in each st to end.

Fasten off. **Do not** turn work.

Rejoin yarn to right-hand edge of work, so that you will begin row 17 at the same edge as you began row 16.

Row 17 (WS) (double loop st): Repeat row 16, but this time turn work at the end of the row in the usual way.

TO COMPLETE STRIPES

Row 18: 1 standing htr (or ch 2) in first double loop st, 1 htr in each double loop st to end.

Rows 19–86: Repeat rows 2–18 four times.

Rows 87–94: Repeat rows 2–9.

Fasten off and weave in ends.

COLOUR SEQUENCE

Foundation chain: Accent colour (dusky pink).

Astrakhan stripes: Work each astrakhan stripe in an accent colour, starting and finishing with a stripe of the same colour (dusky pink) and using a different colour for each of the remaining four stripes (shades of pink/peach).

Double loop stripes: Use the same neutral colour for all five stripes (grey).

Note: You will be changing colour after every repeat of row 9 (the second row of astrakhan stitch) and after every repeat of row 17 (the second row of double loop stitch).

STOCKHOLM

The ombré effect – gradually shading from one colour to another – works perfectly for blankets. I feel it works best with a repetitive stitch pattern, so I have used blanket stitch – what's in a name? – which never fails to deliver a simple yet stunning surface.

SKILL LEVEL

Intermediate

SIZE

Approx. 60 x 100cm (24 x 40in)

YARN

Aran-weight cotton yarn in 6 toning colours from light to dark:
- Off-white – 188m (205yd)
- Light grey – 188m (205yd)
- Light blue – 188m (205yd)
- Dark blue – 188m (205yd)
- Dark grey – 188m (205yd)

HOOK

5mm

TIPS

- In order to create an ombré effect, choose tones of colour that shade into each other, graduating from light to dark.
- As a variation on the colour pattern, try working from a very deep to a thin stripe, making each new stripe slightly less deep than the previous one.

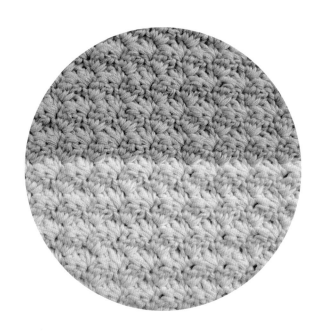

PATTERN

Multiple: 3 sts + 1, plus 2 for foundation chain.

Foundation chain: Ch 90 + 1 + 2 (or adapt to desired width of blanket).

Row 1: Skip first 2 ch from hook (counts as 1 dc), 2 tr in next ch, skip 2 ch, *[1 dc, 2 tr] in next ch, skip 2 ch; repeat from * to last ch, 1 dc in last ch. (30 [1 dc, 2 tr] groups)

Row 2: Ch 2 (counts as 1 dc), 2 tr in first dc, *skip 2 tr, [1 dc, 2 tr] in next dc; repeat from * to last 3 sts, skip 2 sts, 1 dc in last st.

Rows 3–100: Repeat row 2.

Note: When changing colour at beginning of row, work 1 standing dc (or sl st, ch 2) and 2 tr in first dc, then continue as set.

Fasten off and weave in ends.

COLOUR SEQUENCE

Change colours after every 20 rows, working the foundation chain and first stripe in your lightest colour and finishing with a stripe in your darkest colour. In this example, the colour sequence is:

Foundation chain: Off-white.

Rows 1–20: Off-white (20 rows).

Rows 21–40: Light grey (20 rows).

Rows 41–60: Light blue (20 rows).

Rows 61–80: Dark blue (20 rows).

Rows 81–100: Dark grey (20 rows).

CHART

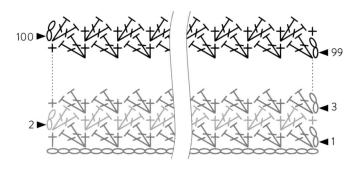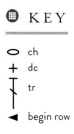

⊞ **KEY**

O ch
+ dc
† tr
◄ begin row

ST PETERSBURG

It is with good reason that most people who come across this stitch pattern – arcade stitch – fall for it. It is reminiscent of shell stitches, but has its own distinct character, being both solid and lacy at the same time. Once you get the hang of the pattern, it is a delight to work.

SKILL LEVEL

Easy

SIZE

Approx. 60 x 90cm (24 x 35in)

YARN

Aran-weight cotton yarn in 1 neutral colour and 4 accent colours:

- Off-white – 300m (328yd)
- Mustard – 75m (82yd)
- Beige – 75m (82yd)
- Green – 75m (82yd)
- Brown – 75m (82yd)

HOOK

5mm

TIPS

Instead of a border, this blanket is finished with one extra row of arcade stitch along the bottom to give the blanket a shell-shaped edge at both top and bottom. However, instead of working just one row of edging, you could position the foundation chain so that it runs across the centre of the blanket and create a mirrored pattern by working the same number of rows on both sides of the foundation chain.

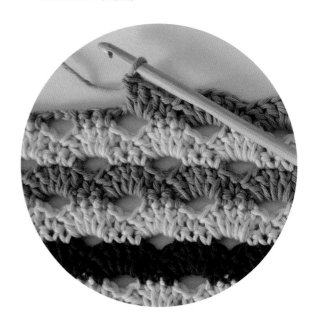

CHART

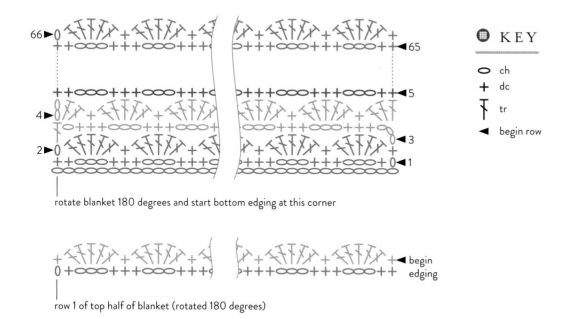

rotate blanket 180 degrees and start bottom edging at this corner

row 1 of top half of blanket (rotated 180 degrees)

KEY

- ○ ch
- + dc
- ⊤ tr
- ◄ begin row

PATTERN

Multiple: 6 sts + 1, plus 1 for foundation chain.

Foundation chain: Ch 90 + 1 + 1 (or adapt to desired width of blanket).

Row 1: Skip first 2 ch from hook (counts as 1 dc), 1 dc in next ch, ch 3, skip 3 ch, *1 dc in each of next 3 ch, ch 3, skip 3 ch; repeat from * to last 2 ch, 1 dc in each of last 2 ch. (15 ch-3 sps)

Row 2: Ch 1 (counts as 1 dc), skip first dc, *skip 1 dc, 5 tr in ch-3 sp (shell made), skip 1 dc, 1 dc in next dc; repeat from * to end. (15 shells)

Row 3: 1 standing tr (or ch 2) in first dc, ch 1, *1 dc in each of centre 3 tr of next shell, ch 3; repeat from * to last shell, 1 dc in each of centre 3 tr of last shell, skip last tr, ch 1, 1 tr in last st.

Row 4: Ch 2 (counts as 1 tr) and 2 tr in first tr (half-shell made), skip first ch and dc, 1 dc in next dc, *skip 1 dc, 5 tr in ch-3 sp (shell made), skip 1 dc, 1 dc in next dc; repeat from * to last dc, skip last dc and next ch, 3 tr in next st (half-shell made). (14 shells and 2 half-shells)

Row 5: 1 standing dc (or sl st, ch 1) in first tr, 1 dc in next tr, ch 3, *1 dc in each of centre 3 tr of next shell, ch 3; repeat from * to last half-shell, skip first tr of last half-shell, 1 dc in each of last 2 sts.

Row 6–66: Repeat rows 2–5, ending with a row 2.

Fasten off and weave in ends.

BOTTOM EDGING

Rotate the blanket so that row 1 is at the top and join yarn to top-right corner dc. Repeat row 2, starting with 1 standing dc (or sl st, ch 1) and working the stitches over the foundation chain and into the dc and ch-3 sps of row 1.

Fasten off and weave in ends.

COLOUR SEQUENCE

Foundation chain: Accent colour.

Rows 1–2: Accent colour (2 rows).

Rows 3–4: Neutral colour (2 rows).

Continue changing colours after every two rows, alternating two rows of accent colour with two rows of neutral colour throughout. Use each of the 4 accent colours in sequence – here, mustard, beige, green and brown, finished with a final stripe of mustard.

Bottom edging: Neutral colour (1 row).

BUENOS AIRES

This is an uncomplicated pattern but it has a surprisingly interesting texture. The colourful tassel fringes add a whimsical and cheerful touch.

SKILL LEVEL

Easy

SIZE

Approx. 65 x 90cm (25 x 35in), excluding tassels

YARN

Aran-weight cotton yarn in 1 neutral colour and as many accent colours as you wish:

• Off-white – 600m (656yd)

• Accent colours – 375m (410yd) in total

HOOK

5mm

TIPS

• To create more texture, experiment by crocheting ch-3 spaces instead of ch-2 spaces on the accent colour stripes.

• This pattern would work very well with a subtle ombré colour plan. Work all of the deeper stripes (treble crochet rows) in one colour (just like the off-white stripes in the blanket shown), but work the thin stripes in toning colours ranging from a light to a very dark hue – for example, multiple tones of grey or blue.

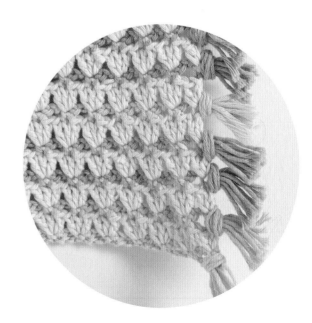

CHART

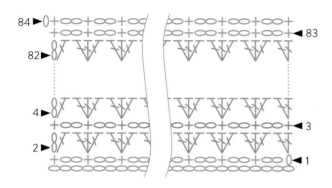

PATTERN

Multiple: 3 sts + 1, plus 1 for foundation chain.

Foundation chain: Ch 108 + 1 + 1 (or adapt to desired width of blanket).

Row 1: 1 dc in 7th ch from hook, *ch 2, skip 2 ch, 1 dc in next ch; repeat from * to end.

Row 2: 1 standing tr (or ch 2) and 1 tr in first dc, 3 tr in each dc to beg ch sp, skip 2 ch, 2 tr in next ch. (35 3-tr groups)

Row 3: 1 standing dc (or sl st, ch 1) in first tr, *ch 2, skip 2 sts, 1 dc in next st; repeat from * to end.

Row 4: 1 standing tr (or ch 2) and 1 tr in first dc, 3 tr in each dc to last st, 2 tr in last st.

Rows 5–83: Repeat rows 3–4, ending with a row 3.

Row 84: Ch 1 (turning ch), 1 dc in first dc, *ch 2, skip 2 ch, 1 dc in next st; repeat from * to end.

Fasten off and weave in ends from the tr rows only (neutral colour).

TASSEL FRINGE

Tie a knot in each yarn end at the edge of every narrow stripe (the rows worked in accent colours) to make sure they do not unravel. Add a tassel at each end of every narrow stripe, incorporating the ends of yarn from working the rows into the tassels. Trim the tassels to the same length on each side of the blanket.

COLOUR SEQUENCE

Coloured stripes: Use the same accent colour for the foundation chain and row 1, then use a different accent colour for each narrow stripe (dc-and-ch rows). Finish with the same accent colour for the final two rows.

Neutral stripes: Use off-white for all of the deeper stripes (tr rows).

Tassels: Match the tassel colour to the stripe colour.

ACAPULCO

There is a lot going on stitchwise in this pattern, so I have kept the colour scheme classic and basic – black and white, with a mint border for a touch of colour. The boldly contrasting colours provide beautiful definition to the geometric pattern. The surprising detail is that the pattern is mirrored, with the top and bottom halves of the blanket being worked on both sides of the foundation chain, which runs through the centre of the blanket.

SKILL LEVEL

Advanced

SIZE

Approx. 60 x 90cm (24 x 35in)

YARN

Aran-weight cotton yarn in 3 colours:

• Black – 300m (328yd)
• Off-white – 300m (328yd)
• Mint green – 150m (164yd)

HOOK

5mm

TIPS

• This is a mirrored pattern, starting at the central black stripe. You begin by making the top half of the blanket, and then repeat the pattern on the other side of the foundation chain to make a bottom half that is identical to the top.

• Although the blanket features stripes with several different stitch patterns, the colour sequence is not difficult to remember. Simply work 4 rows white, 4 rows black and 4 rows white on either side of the central black stripe, then continue alternating 1 row black and 1 row white to complete the blanket.

• I have started each border round with a standing stitch and finished the round with an invisible join, but you can begin each round with a turning chain and finish with a slip stitch join if you prefer (see page 124).

BLANKET CHART

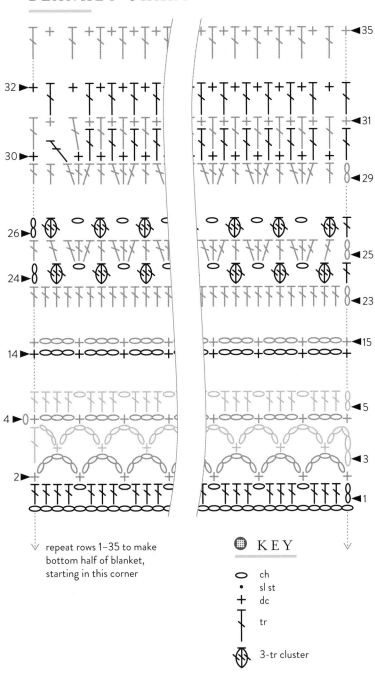

repeat rows 1–35 to make bottom half of blanket, starting in this corner

⊕ KEY

- ◯ ch
- • sl st
- + dc
- † tr
- 3-tr cluster
- ◄ begin row or round

BORDER CHART

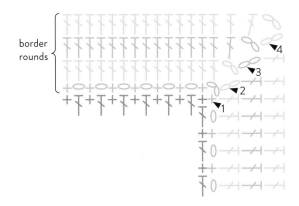

border rounds

PATTERN

Multiple: 4 sts + 1, plus 2 for foundation chain.

Foundation chain: Ch 84 + 1 + 2 (or adapt to desired width of blanket).

FIRST HALF OF BLANKET

Row 1: Skip first 3 ch from hook (counts as 1 tr), *1 tr in each of next 3 ch, ch 1, skip 1 ch; repeat from * to last 4 ch, 1 tr in each of last 4 ch. (20 ch-1 sps)

Row 2: 1 standing dc (or sl st, ch 1) in first tr, [ch 5, 1 dc] in each ch-1 sp to last 4 sts, ch 5, skip 3 sts, 1 dc in last st. (21 ch-5 sps)

Row 3: [Ch 5, 1 dc] in each ch-5 sp to end, ch 3, 1 tr in last st.

Row 4: Ch 1 (turning ch), 1 dc in first tr, [ch 3, 1 dc] in each ch-5 sp to end, working last dc in 3rd ch of beg ch.

Row 5: Ch 2 (counts as 1 tr), skip first dc, 3 tr in first ch-3 sp, *ch 1, skip 1 dc, 3 tr in next ch-3 sp; repeat from * to last st, 1 tr in last st.

Rows 6–13: Repeat rows 2–5.

Row 14: 1 standing dc (or sl st, ch 1) in first tr, *[ch 3, 1 dc] in each ch-1 sp to last 4 sts, ch 3, skip 3 sts, 1 dc in last st.

Row 15: 1 standing dc (or sl st, ch 1) in first dc, *ch 3, skip ch-3 sp, 1 dc in next st; repeat from * to end.

Rows 16–22: Repeat row 15.

Row 23: 1 standing tr (or ch 2) in first st, *3 tr in next ch-3 sp, 1 tr in next st; repeat from * to end. (85 tr)

Row 24: 1 standing tr (or ch 2) in first tr, skip 1 tr, 3-tr cluster in next tr, *ch 1, skip 3 tr, 3-tr cluster in next tr; repeat from * to last 2 sts, skip 1 st, 1 tr in last st. (21 clusters)

Row 25: 1 standing tr (or ch 2) in first tr, *1 tr in next cluster, 3 tr in ch-1 sp; repeat from * to last cluster, 1 tr in last cluster, 1 tr in last st. (83 tr)

Row 26: 1 standing tr (or ch 2) in first tr, *3-tr cluster in next tr, ch 1, skip 3 tr; repeat from * to last 2 sts, 3-tr cluster in next st, 1 tr in last st.

Rows 27–29: Repeat row 25, then 26, then 25 again.

Row 30: 1 standing dc (or sl st, ch 1) in first tr, skip 1 tr, *1 tr in next tr, 1 dc in next tr; repeat from * to last st, 1 tr in last st.

Row 31: 1 standing dc (or sl st, ch 1) in first tr, *1 tr in next dc, 1 dc in next tr; repeat from * to last st, 1 tr in last st.

Row 32: 1 standing dc (or sl st, ch 1) in first tr, *1 tr in next dc, 1 dc in next tr; repeat from * to last st, 1 tr in last st.

Rows 33–35: Repeat row 31, then 32, then 31 again.

SECOND HALF OF BLANKET

Rotate blanket so that foundation chain is at the top. Join yarn to top-right corner stitch and repeat rows 2–35 to mirror first half of blanket.

Fasten off and weave in ends.

BORDER

Start in top-right corner st with a standing dc (or sl st, ch 1); use a standing tr (or ch 2) to start rounds 2–4.

Round 1: Work *[1 dc, ch 2, 1 dc] in corner st, ch 1, skip 1 st, [1 dc in next st, ch 1, skip 1 st] to next corner, [1 dc, ch 2, 1 dc] in corner st. Working along side edge of blanket, ch 1, skip 1 row, [1 dc in side of next row, ch 1, skip 1 row] to next corner; repeat from * once. Join.

Round 2: Work [1 tr, ch 2, 1 tr] in each corner ch-2 sp, and 1 tr in each dc and ch-1 sp around sides. Join.

Rounds 3–4: Repeat round 2.

Fasten off and weave in ends.

COLOUR SEQUENCE

Foundation chain: Black.

Row 1: Black (1 row).

Rows 2–5: White (4 rows).

Rows 6–9: Black (4 rows).

Rows 10–13: White (4 rows).

Rows 14–35: Alternate 1 row black and 1 row white (22 rows).

Second half of blanket: Repeat colour sequence of rows 2–35.

Border: Mint green (4 rounds).

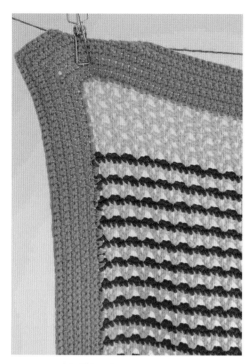

BORDERS

Some blankets are perfect as they are without an additional border, while with others the border is an integral part of the design – the Jaipur (left) and Casablanca (below left) blankets, for example – and in some cases a border is simply the cherry on top.

REASONS TO ADD A BORDER

There can be a number of practical reasons for adding a border.

- You can use a border to straighten up a wonky blanket with uneven sides or to add extra durability to the blanket.

- A border can provide an extra space to weave in ends.

- Adding a border is an excellent way to enlarge or otherwise adjust the size of a blanket. So if you are happy with the length of the blanket but feel it should be a bit wider, simply add some extra border rows on the sides to make it wider.

- If you are not 100 per cent happy with the colours of your blanket or would just like to add more colour, then a border is the perfect place to adjust the colour plan without unravelling a whole blanket.

- Or if you feel the blanket turned out a bit boring? Add a frivolous border! Blanket too frilly? Add a stern border!

TECHNIQUES FOR
A TIDY BORDER

A border pattern can often be worked directly on to the blanket, but sometimes the blanket needs tidying up, or you may just need a regular stitch pattern around the edges to act as a baseline on to which you can work the main border pattern.

- The most common base for a border is often just a round of double crochet or treble crochet stitches around all four sides of the blanket. However, this is not always the most pretty or effective base. It can sometimes look a bit messy, especially on the sides where the rows start and end, and especially when using a different colour for the border. It can also cause the edges of the blanket to ruffle or cup.

- In most cases I prefer to make a baseline by alternating double crochet and chain stitches. This often looks much tidier, because the chains make a straighter side and are easier to block in the right shape. Plus it often ensures a better drape. If neat sides are not an issue, you can try alternating treble crochet and chain stitches as a baseline, which gives an elegant lacy look.

- If the blanket looks a bit messy on the sides, another good idea is to straighten it with a baseline using a colour that matches the one(s) in the blanket, and then change to another colour for the main border pattern. This way the contrasting border stitches can be worked more regularly and the result will be tidier.

- Before adding the 'official' border pattern, I often crochet quite a few rounds of double, half treble or treble crochet around the baseline. It is a perfect and easy way to add size to the blanket, and the border will appear to be framing the blanket, making it shine like the right frame does for a painting.

SPECIAL CONSIDERATIONS
WHEN WORKING WITH STRIPES

You need to consider the stripes when deciding to add a border and, if so, which border and where to add it.

- A border on four sides can interfere with the stripe pattern because it 'breaks' the stripe design. In some cases this is fine and the border works as the perfect frame to highlight the stripes, but in other cases it does not.

- One way to deal with this is to only add a border in the same direction as the stripes.

- Another option is to work 'with' the stripes, such as in the Buenos Aires blanket (below). A fringe of short pompom-esque tassels in the colours of the stripes (pompoms would work too) are added only along the side edges of the blanket. This enhances the stripe effect and gives a lovely finishing touch.

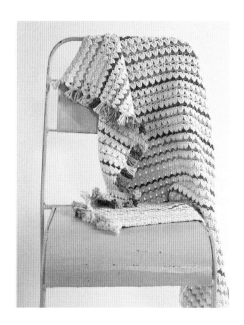

CROCHET BORDERS

In addition to the borders featured in some of the blanket designs, this section provides five more crochet border patterns that you can use to frame your blankets. They are all made using a 3.5mm hook and 4ply-weight cotton yarn in two neutral colours. You can make each border in a single colour or as many colours as you like, using the colour palette of your blanket as inspiration. Here are some tips for working the border patterns:

• The samples and charts start with a round of chain stitches as the base for the main border pattern. This is simply because they are not attached to a blanket. Unless you want to work the border separately and then sew it on, you should omit this round of chains and work the first round of the main border pattern directly on to your blanket (or on to the baseline you have added around your blanket – see 'Techniques for a tidy border' on page 93).

• If you work round 1 directly on to the blanket without an additional baseline round, then remember that when the pattern instructs you to work into a stitch, this could in fact mean that you will be working into the side of a stitch (along the sides of the blanket where you started/ended your rows). If your blanket edge or baseline round

includes chains, you may also be working some of the first round of border stitches into chain spaces. This will depend on the pattern of your blanket, so adapt the first round of the border pattern accordingly.

• For best results, always cut the yarn after finishing each round and use an invisible join (rather than a slip stitch join), then start the new round with a standing stitch (rather than a turning chain). Refer to page 124 for more information.

• Be creative with the stitch count! Does your blanket not have the exact matching stitch count for the border of your choice? There are a couple of tricks to fix that. If the border pattern says to skip stitches, try skipping more or fewer stitches, or smuggle in a few extra stitches in the first round of the border. Another trick is to crochet stitches together (dc2tog or tr2tog) if the border pattern needs fewer stitches than the blanket provides.

• To prevent the border from ruffling (becoming too loose and forming ruffles) or cupping (becoming too tight and lifting up to form a cup shape), you can try switching to a smaller hook (in case of ruffling) or to a bigger one (in case of cupping). Or try one of the tricks above to adjust the stitch count.

TIP

The border patterns can be used on their own to make a lovely retro valance, in which case you would start with a foundation round of chain stitches, as shown on the charts.

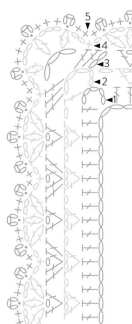

PICOT SHELLS

Note: The baseline multiple is 6 sts + 3 along sides, plus 1 st at each corner. Use colour A for rounds 1–4 and colour B for round 5. Work first st of rounds 1–3 as a standing tr (or ch 2) and first st of rounds 4–5 as a standing dc (or sl st, ch 1). If preferred, skip round 1 and work round 2 directly on to blanket.

Special stitches: Corner CL (cluster) = [(tr2tog, ch 3) twice, tr2tog] in ch sp.

Side CL (cluster) = [(tr2tog, ch 2) twice, tr2tog] in ch sp.

Picot-3 = ch 3, sl st in tr2tog.

Round 1: Starting in any corner st of blanket, *[1 tr, ch 3, 1 tr] in corner st, 1 tr in each st to next corner; repeat from * three times. Join.

Round 2: Starting in any corner sp, *[1 tr, ch 3, 1 tr] in corner sp, ch 1, skip 2 tr, **[1 tr, ch 2, 1 tr] in next tr, ch 1, skip 2 tr; repeat from ** to next corner. Repeat from * three times. Join.

Round 3: Starting in any corner sp, *[3 tr, ch 3, 3 tr] in corner sp, skip ch-1 sp, **[1 tr, ch 1, 1 tr] in next ch-2 sp, skip ch-1 sp, [2 tr, ch 1, 2 tr] in next ch-2 sp; repeat from ** to next corner. Repeat from * three times. Join.

Round 4: Starting in 3rd tr of first 3-tr group in any corner, *1 dc in 3rd tr, ch 2, corner CL in corner ch-3 sp, ch 2, 1 dc in next tr, **ch 1, side CL in next ch-1 sp, ch 1, 1 dc in next ch-1 sp; repeat from ** to next corner. Repeat from * three times. Join.

Round 5: Starting in first ch-2 sp of any corner, *2 dc in ch-2 sp, [picot-3, 3 dc in next ch-3 sp] twice, picot-3, 2 dc in next ch-2 sp (corner made), **1 dc in next ch-1 sp, [picot-3, 2 dc in next ch-2 sp] twice, picot-3, 1 dc in next ch-1 sp; repeat from ** to next corner. Repeat from * three times. Join.

Fasten off and weave in ends.

○ KEY

○	ch
•	sl st
+	dc
┬	tr
⋀	tr2tog
⋀	picot-3
◄	begin round

KEY

○   ch

⊤   tr

◄   begin round

TRADITIONAL STITCH

Note: The baseline multiple is 4 sts + 1 along sides, plus 1 st at each corner. Use colour A for round 1 and colour B for round 2, then alternate colours on every round. Work first st of each round as a standing tr (or ch 2).

Round 1: Starting in any corner st of blanket, *[1 tr, ch 2, 1 tr] in corner st, 1 tr in each of next 2 sts, ch 1, skip 1 st, [1 tr in each of next 3 sts, ch 1, skip 1 st] to last 2 sts before next corner, 1 tr in each of last 2 sts; repeat from * three times. Join.

Round 2: Starting in first ch-1 sp after any corner, *[3 tr, ch 1] in each ch-1 sp to next corner, [3 tr, ch 2, 3 tr] in corner sp, ch 1; repeat from * three times. Join.

Round 3–6: Repeat row 2 four times (or for as many rounds as you like).

Fasten off and weave in ends.

FLOATING FLOWERS

Note: The baseline multiple is 6 sts + 2 along sides, plus 1 st at each corner. Use colour A for round 1 and colour B for round 2. Work first st of round 1 as a standing tr (or ch 2) and first st of round 2 as a standing dc (or sl st, ch 1). If preferred, skip round 1 and work round 2 directly on to blanket. The border alternates flowers with short and long stems, with 1 dc between flowers along sides of blanket. For a less dense border, work more dc between the flowers.

Special stitch: Flower = sl st in 5th ch from hook (ring made), *[ch 3, 2 tr, ch 3, sl st] in ring (petal made); repeat from * 3 times (flower completed).

Round 1: Starting in any corner st of blanket, *[1 tr, ch 3, 1 tr] in corner st, 1 tr in each st to next corner; repeat from * three times. Join.

Round 2: Starting in first tr after any corner sp, *1 dc in each of first 2 tr, ch 8, flower, ch 3, 1 dc in each of next 3 tr, ch 14, flower, ch 9, 1 dc in each of next 3 tr; repeat from * to last 2 tr before next corner sp, ch 8, flower, ch 3, 1 dc in each of next 2 tr. Continuing to alternate short and long stems as set, work three flowers in corner ch-3 sp, omitting the extra dc between flower stems (so work only 6 dc in the corner sp). Repeat from * three times. Join.

Fasten off and weave in ends.

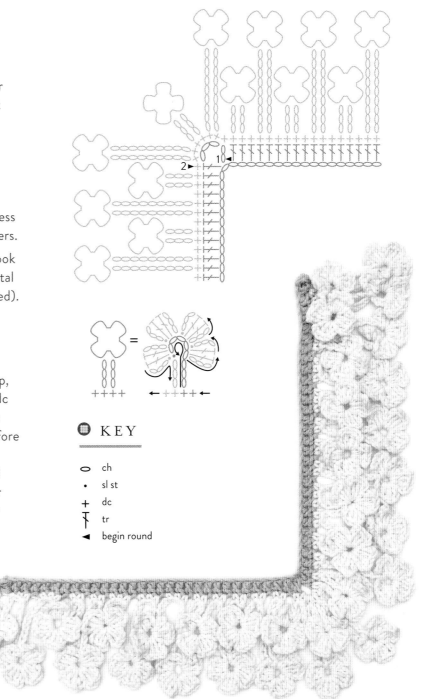

⊞ KEY

○	ch
•	sl st
+	dc
⊺	tr
◄	begin round

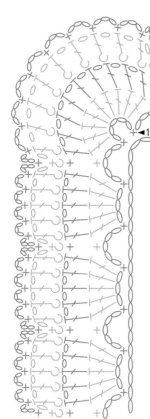

RUFFLE SHELLS

Note: The baseline multiple is 6 sts + 2 along sides, plus 1 st at each corner. Use colour A for rounds 1–3 and colour B for rounds 4–5. If you wish to change the colour plan, the design looks best using a different colour for rounds 3 and 4 so that the back post stitches of round 4 create an interlaced colour effect around the sts of round 3. Work first st of each round as a standing dc (or sl st, ch 1), working around back post on round 4.

Round 1: Starting in any corner st of blanket, *[1 dc, ch 5, 1 dc] in corner st, **ch 5, skip 2 sts, 1 dc in next st, ch 3, skip 2 sts, 1 dc in next st; repeat from ** to last 2 sts before next corner, ch 5, skip last 2 sts. Repeat from * three times. Join.

Round 2: Starting in last ch-5 sp before any corner ch-5 sp, *1 dc in ch-5 sp before corner, 9 tr in corner sp, **1 dc in next ch-5 sp, 5 tr in next ch-3 sp; repeat from ** to last ch-5 sp before next corner. Repeat from * three times. Join.

Round 3: Starting in last dc before any corner 9-tr group, *1 dc in dc before corner, [1 tr in next tr, ch 1] 8 times, 1 tr in next tr, **1 dc in next dc, [1 tr in next tr, ch 1] 4 times, 1 tr in next tr; repeat from ** to last dc before next corner. Repeat from * three times. Join.

Round 4: Starting in last dc before any corner tr group, *1 BPdc in dc before corner, ch 1, [1 BPtr in next tr, ch 1] 9 times, **1 BPdc in next dc, ch 1, [1 BPtr in next tr, ch 1] 5 times; repeat from ** to last dc before next corner. Repeat from * three times. Join.

Round 5: Starting in any BPdc or BPtr, [1 dc, ch 3] in each dc and tr around. Join.

Fasten off and weave in ends.

KEY

o	ch
+	dc
⌂	BPdc
⊤	tr
⊤	BPtr
◄	begin round

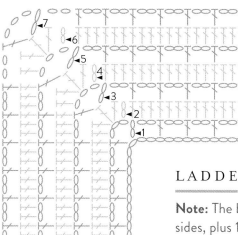

KEY

- ○   ch
- ⊤   tr
- ◄   begin round

LADDER LACE

Note: The baseline multiple is 3 sts + 2 along sides, plus 1 st at each corner. Use colour A for rounds 1–2 and colour B for rounds 3–7. Work first st of each round as a standing tr (or ch 2).

Round 1: Starting in any corner st of blanket, *[1 tr, ch 3, 1 tr] in corner st, ch 2, skip 2 sts, **1 tr in next st, ch 2, skip 2 sts; repeat from ** to next corner. Repeat from * three times. Join.

Round 2: Starting in any corner ch-3 sp, *5 tr in corner sp, 1 tr in each tr and 2 tr in each ch-2 sp to next corner; repeat from * three times. Join.

Round 3: Starting in centre tr of any corner 5-tr group, repeat round 1.

Rounds 4–7: Repeat rounds 2–3 twice.

Fasten off and weave in ends.

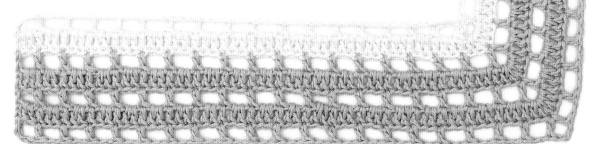

NON-CROCHET TRIMS

Remember that a border does not have to be crocheted in order to add some oomph to your blanket. Here are a few ideas to get you started, but the only limit is your imagination.

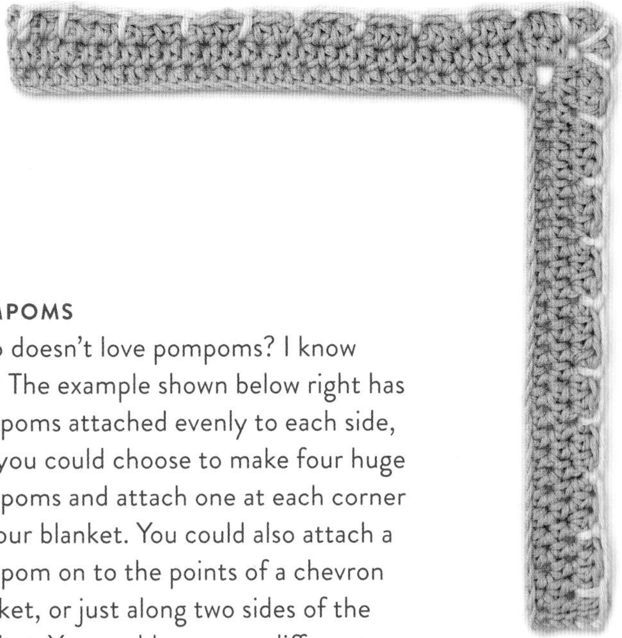

BLANKET STITCH

A simple and sophisticated finish is to sew blanket stitch around the edges of your blanket. For a more pronounced blanket stitch edge (as shown above right), use a chunkier yarn than you have used for the rest of the blanket. This has the added benefit of covering up any slightly wonky sides on the blanket.

TASSELS

Short, long, tied together, beaded – there are so many possible variations. Shown below left is a basic example just to give you a taste.

POMPOMS

Who doesn't love pompoms? I know I do! The example shown below right has pompoms attached evenly to each side, but you could choose to make four huge pompoms and attach one at each corner of your blanket. You could also attach a pompom on to the points of a chevron blanket, or just along two sides of the blanket. You could even use different sizes of pompoms on the same blanket, or leave a long tail so that they dangle from the blanket. It can also be really nice to attach them not only to a border, but also to the front of the blanket. If the blanket is for heavy use and will be washed often, you could consider attaching the pompoms with safety pins or simple knots, so that you can take them off before washing.

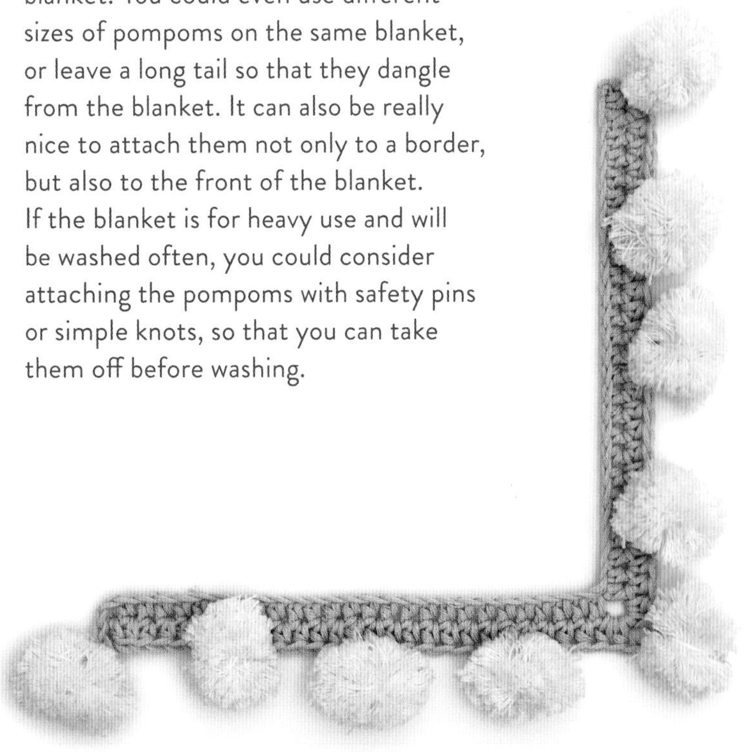

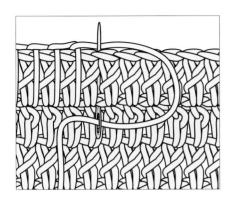

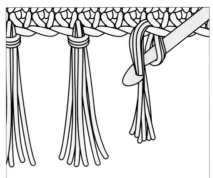

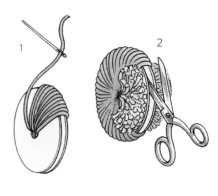

SEWING BLANKET STITCH

Turn the work to embroider the line of blanket stitch from left to right. Using a yarn needle, bring the needle through to the front on the left-hand edge of the blanket and form a loop with the yarn. Decide how deep you want the stitches to be – for example, one row deep. Insert the needle into this row, a short distance to the right, and bring it out directly above, on the edge of the blanket, inside the loop. Pull through. Continue working L-shaped blanket stitches around the edge. Fasten off with a small stitch over the last loop.

ADDING A TASSEL FRINGE

To add a simple fringe of tassels to your blanket, cut a rectangle of cardboard about 2.5cm (1in) wider than the depth of fringe you want. Wind the yarn around the cardboard as many times as required. Cut along one edge to make lots of strands of the same length.

Decide on the spacing you want for your fringe, and how many strands to use for each tassel. Fold the strands in half. Insert a crochet hook through the blanket from back to front and pull the loop of strands through. Then catch the ends of the strands and pull them through the loop. Repeat as required, taking care to attach all tassels from the same side of the blanket because the tassels look different from the back and front. Lay the fringe flat and trim all the tassels to the same length.

MAKING A POMPOM

1 Kits of plastic frames are available to help you produce traditional fluffy pompoms, but if you don't have one, simply cut out two rings of cardboard. Place the rings together and use a yarn needle to wrap yarn around them. Starting new lengths of yarn at the outside edge, continue until the rings are tightly covered.

2 Insert the blade of a pair of scissors between the rings and cut the yarn around the outside edge.

3 Tie a length of yarn around the pompom between the rings. Knot the yarn tightly, slip the rings off and trim the pompom to neaten. Use the ends of yarn from the tie for attaching the pompom to the blanket.

CHAPTER 2

PROJECTS

PORTO RUG

Many of the blankets in this book are perfect for upsizing to a cosy rug. Here, I adapted the Marrakech blanket by using bright pastels and alternating two depths of stripes. Otherwise, the basic pattern remains unaltered and has the same advantage as the original blanket – a nifty technique for changing colours neatly that reduces the number of ends to weave in enormously.

SKILL LEVEL

Intermediate

SIZE

Approx. 100 x 150cm (40 x 60in)

YARN

Super chunky-weight cotton blend yarn in 1 neutral colour and as many bright colours as you wish:

- Pearl white – 672m (735yd)
- Bright colours (I used 10 colours) – 912m (998yd) in total

HOOK

10mm

TIPS

You can vary this pattern almost endlessly. For instance, you can make very wide vertical colour panels, or alternate between wide and narrow panels. You can also use more than three colours on each row – ideal if you prefer to make a square rug.

PATTERN

Use the Marrakech pattern (page 32), and the same hook size throughout, with the following changes:

Foundation chain: Ch 25 in a bright colour (A), ch 25 in off-white (B), ch 27 in another bright colour (C).

Each row: Work 25 tr in each colour (instead of 30).

Horizontal stripes: Change colours after every seven rows and then three rows to create alternating deep and narrow stripes. Use pearl white for the narrow stripes in the outer vertical panels, and a different bright colour for each deep stripe. Reverse this in the centre vertical panel – off-white deep stripes and colourful narrow stripes.

CHIANG MAI POTHOLDER AND DISH TOWEL

Stripes are ideal for making a retro-style potholder and dish towel. If you choose a pattern that creates a dense fabric like this one, you will probably not even need to make a reverse side. If you pick a lacy pattern, make a second piece using a pattern that creates a dense fabric and sew it to the reverse.

SKILL LEVEL

Intermediate

SIZE

Potholder: approx. 21 x 21cm (8¼ x 8¼in)

Dish towel: approx. 42 x 42cm (16½ x 16½in)

YARN

Aran-weight cotton yarn in 2 colours for potholder:

• Mustard or blue – 20m (22yd)
• Pink – 25m (28yd)

Aran-weight cotton yarn in 4 colours for dish towel:

• Off-white – 38m (41yd)
• Pink – 75m (82yd)
• Blue – 20m (22yd)
• Mustard – 19m (21yd)

HOOK

5mm for potholder

6mm for dish towel (for a looser drape)

PATTERN

Use the Lisbon pattern (page 56), and the same hook size throughout, with the following changes:

Potholder: Ch 30 and work 23 rows, alternating 1 row mustard or blue with 1 row off-white.

Dish towel: Ch 52 and work 37 rows, alternating 1 row off-white with 1 row pink/blue/mustard, using each of the three colours in sequence.

Border (both projects): Work in pink, adding a hanging loop as follows:

Row 1: Ch 10 (instead of 3) at the top-left corner to create a hanging loop.

Row 2: Work 13 dc into the ch-10 hanging loop.

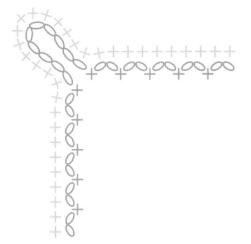

KEY

O ch
+ dc

SHIRAZ CUSHION

This cushion is the perfect companion for the Casablanca blanket. The front and back of the cushion are different from each other, but both are derived from the same blanket pattern. Like the blanket, the cushion has the advantage of very few yarn ends to weave in – plus it's a pattern that just can't go wrong!

SKILL LEVEL

Intermediate

SIZE

Approx. 45cm (18in) wide x 40cm (16in) high

YARN

Aran-weight cotton yarn in as many colours as you wish:

• Total quantity – 338m (369yd)

HOOK

4mm for front panel

6mm for back panel

TIPS

I have used a smaller hook for the front panel in order to create a dense fabric with minimal show-through of the cushion pad inside. I have used a larger hook for the back to maintain the 'shabby' boucherouite effect, but you can use the smaller hook if you prefer and adjust the pattern to match the size of the front panel.

PATTERN

Starting and ending each row of a new colour with generous tails of yarn, use the Casablanca pattern (page 68) with the following changes:

Front panel: Following the centre panel pattern, ch 72 and work 42 rows, changing colour for every row.

Back panel: Following the side panel pattern, ch 55 and work 25 rows, changing colour approx. two-thirds of the way along the first row (after 36 sts in the cushion shown). Match this colour change on each subsequent row – so two-thirds along each right-side row, and one-third along each wrong-side row. Change both colours after every 5 rows to make the horizontal stripes.

ASSEMBLING THE CUSHION

Side edges: Use the ends of yarn to tie the panels together. The front panel will have more ends than the back panel because you have changed colour on every row, so you will need to transfer half of these ends to the back panel in order to tie the panels together. Do this by using a yarn needle to thread the yarn end through the back panel where necessary. There should be sufficient ends for a sturdy join, but you can use extra yarn if needed. Make sure all the ends are tied on the same side and trim them to equal length. You can choose whether you want to have them on the outside, as part of the design, or tucked away on the inside.

Top and bottom edges: Join the top edges together with a simple double crochet seam. Either do the same along the bottom edge or use buttons.

FEZ WALL HANGING

When I made the Oslo blanket, I felt that the pattern would also be perfect for a wall hanging. Here, I have downsized the blanket to make a mini-wall hanging. Moroccan wedding blankets were the inspiration for the white base, with the addition of silver and gold – and sequins for the finishing touch.

SKILL LEVEL

Advanced

SIZE

25 x 60cm (10 x 24in), plus 15cm (6in) fringe

YARN

Super chunky-weight acrylic yarn in 1 colour:
• Off-white – 80m (87yd)

DK-weight cotton/lurex metallic yarn in 2 colours:
• Silver – 130m (142yd)
• Gold – 130m (142yd)

Laceweight polyester yarn with pre-threaded sequins in 1 colour:
• Gold – 30m (33yd)

HOOK

10mm

TIPS

• Work each off-white section of the wall hanging using one strand of off-white yarn held together with one strand of sequin yarn.

• Work the metallic sections using three strands of metallic yarn held together – three strands of silver together, and three strands of gold together – so either buy three balls of each colour, or buy one ball of each and then wind each ball in three smaller balls.

• Another take on this wall hanging would be to crochet it with jute and linen, for a more rustic look.

• You can use a lot of things as a hanger for displaying your wall hanging – a simple branch (like the one in the photograph), around which you could wrap the leftover silver or gold yarn, a copper tube or a piece of bamboo. Make sure whatever you use is a bit wider than the fabric.

PATTERN

Foundation chain: Ch 23 (off-white/sequins).

Main panel: Work the following rows from the Oslo pattern (page 72), using the colours indicated:

- Rows 1–2 (off-white/sequins).
- Rows 7–9 (gold)
- Rows 10–13 (off-white/sequins)
- Row 17 (silver)
- Rows 18 and 2–4 (off-white/sequins)
- Rows 7–9 (gold)
- Rows 10–13 (off-white/sequins)

Decoration: Tie a fringe of off-white tassels along the bottom of the panel, with one gold tassel for contrast. Trim to desired length. If you wish, tie a few gold and silver mini-tassels to the front of the off-white sections.

Attaching to a hanger: Thread a yarn needle with off-white yarn. Hold the hanger alongside the top of the fabric and, starting from the reverse of the fabric, sew the fabric to the hanger with loops of yarn.

SALVADOR BEDSPREAD

This bedspread is an upsized version of the St George's blanket. It is upsized very simply by working longer and more rows using a chunky yarn. Like the original blanket, I chose colours with a retro feel, but a very different palette – inspired by that lovely town in Brazil with its beautifully coloured houses.

SKILL LEVEL

Advanced

SIZE

Approx. 160 x 200cm (63 x 79in)

YARN

Chunky-weight cotton/acrylic yarn in 1 neutral colour and 4 accent colours:

• Cream – 798m (868yd)
• Light pink – 570m (620yd)
• Mid-pink – 570m (620yd)
• Brown – 570m (620yd)
• Dark pink – 570m (620yd)

HOOK

7mm

PATTERN

Use the St George's pattern (page 40), with the following changes:

Foundation chain: Ch 165.

Stripe pattern: Change colour after every four (instead of six) and then two rows, remembering to work the next row of treble crochet after every colour change into the back loops only. Work 94 rows in total.

Colour sequence: Work the foundation chain and every 4-row stripe in an accent colour and every 2-row stripe in the neutral colour. Use each of the 4 accent colours in sequence – here, light pink, mid-pink, brown and dark pink.

CHAPTER 3

TECHNIQUES

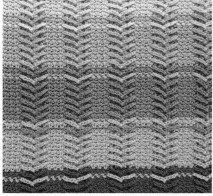

COLOUR ME BEAUTIFUL

Colours define a crochet pattern, and that is certainly the case with stripes. A whole book could be written about that, but I will restrict myself here to the main issues to keep in mind when picking colours and a colour plan for your stripy blankets.

Colour palette

When it comes to which colours to use, you will no doubt have your own preferences. You may love monochrome palettes, black and white, bright colours, sedated hues or, like me, be rather partial to pastels with lots of off-white thrown into the mix. Oftentimes we find ourselves reaching for colours we know we love. However, it does pay off to experiment with colours that are not your first love. Sometimes they complement the other colours perfectly, or make them pop even more. Also, a colour that is not your favourite can get a new look if combined with unexpected colours.

Remember also that the impact of a colour will be affected by how much of it you use. A small stripe of any colour between larger stripes of another colour will have a very different impact – both on itself and on the other colours – than if that colour were used to make the same-size stripe as the other stripes. So when working on a blanket, it can be useful to be flexible. From time to time, question your choices. Try holding a ball of another colour next to your work in progress to see what impact the colour has. Experiment and enjoy!

Stripe colour plan

Be aware that the shape and size of the stripes can be defined by either the stitch pattern or the colours, or by both.

For some patterns, where and how often you change colours is relatively arbitrary, in that it is not dependent on the stitch pattern. For instance, the Marseille blanket (below, far left) is made from scraps and I changed colour for every row, but you could change colour after as many rows as you like – for example, after every five rows to make wider stripes. Alternatively, you could use two colours and alternate one row in each colour. Or just use one colour for the whole blanket – it would still be a stripy blanket, but the stripes would be defined purely by the stitch pattern, not by colour. The possibilities are almost endless, but whichever option you choose, it will have a huge impact on the blanket – without changing a stitch of the pattern.

The Weimar blanket (below, centre left) is in some ways similar to the Marseille. Stitchwise, each row is a repeat of the first, and the stitches are simple solid ones. However, the outcome is a very different blanket because of the use of colour, with the Weimar having both wide and narrow colour stripes, plus vertical ones created by the moss stitch pattern.

The Bruges and Havana blankets (below, centre right and far right) have in common that they consist of lacy, fairly wide stripes, with the stitch pattern repeating after every few rows. However, in the monochrome Bruges blanket the stripes are only defined by the stitch pattern, whereas in the Havana the stripes are highlighted by changing colour for each repeat of the pattern. The latter does not have to be the case, though. For example, you could make the colour stripes twice as big as the stitch-pattern stripes by only changing colour after every two repeats of the stitch pattern.

Downsizing or upsizing

There are two main ways to change the size of your blanket, but be aware that these may have an impact on the finished blanket beyond simply altering the size.

The first method is to follow the same pattern, but use a finer or chunkier yarn and hook. However, be aware that the size of hook I have used for a particular weight of yarn may be smaller or larger than usual for that yarn weight in order to achieve the desired texture and drape using a particular stitch pattern. Because of this, it is important to make a test swatch to try out different yarn and hook combinations until you achieve a result you are happy with. This will also help you to calculate the final size of your project.

The second method is to shorten or extend the pattern, using the multiple information provided to make the foundation chain shorter or longer (see page 118), and working fewer or more rows. When doing this, it is important to think beforehand what the consequences will be for the look of the blanket. For example, if you are upsizing a pattern in which the colours are changed after every five rows, the photographed example may have relatively wide colour stripes, but in a bigger blanket these stripes will look narrower. This may be fine, but if you want to keep the same look as the original smaller blanket, you would need to change colours after more than five rows – for instance, after every ten rows.

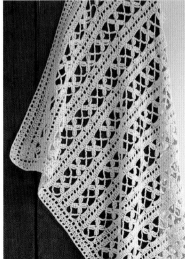

PATTERN NOTES

Before picking up your hook, I strongly recommend that you read these notes. They will help you to get a good understanding of the blanket patterns and your choices about how to crochet them.

Multiples

Each pattern specifies the length of foundation chain required to make the size of blanket shown in the photographs, but at the beginning of the pattern you will also find the pattern 'multiple'. The number of chains to make for the foundation chain is provided as a multiple of a specific number so that you can easily upsize or downsize the design to your own requirements. A specified number of extra chains is often added after the multiple calculation to balance the design and/or to allow for the turning chain on the first row.

In this book the multiple is expressed as follows, for example: 'a multiple of 3 + 2, plus 1 for the foundation chain'. This means that you should work a multiple of three chains – 3, 6, 9 and so on – and then add an extra two chains to balance the design – 3 + 2, 6 + 2, 9 + 2. Finally, you should add one more chain to allow for the turning chain required for the first row – 3 + 2 + 1, 6 + 2 + 1, 9 + 2 + 1.

Working in rows and rounds

Unless instructed otherwise, always turn the work at the end of each row of the blanket pattern. Don't turn the work when working borders in rounds unless instructed to do so (see also page 124).

Turning chains

Turning chains are used at the beginning of a row (or round) to bring the hook up to the correct height to work the following stitches. I recommend the usual one turning chain for double crochet and two chains for half treble crochet, but for taller stitches I prefer to work one fewer chain than usual in order to create a neater edge – so two chains for treble crochet (instead of three) and so on.

Sometimes the turning chain acts as a substitute for the first stitch of the row, and the pattern will tell you if this is the case – for example, 'ch 2 (counts as 1 tr)'. Unless instructed otherwise, work the last stitch of the following row into the top chain of the substitute stitch.

Charts

Each blanket chart includes several stitch repeats along each row. The wavy vertical lines indicate that you should continue working the stitch repeat as set across to the end of the row. Dashed lines indicate where rows are to be repeated; refer to the written pattern for instructions on which rows to repeat. Border charts include at least one corner, several stitches along the top and/or bottom row and several row ends.

Whenever the written pattern indicates that you have the option of using a standing dc to begin a row (or round), the chart shows a dc symbol with no turning chain. When there is the option of using a standing htr or taller stitch, the chart shows the usual turning chains.

Changing colours

Refer to the 'Colour sequence' list at the end of the blanket pattern for when to change colour. You can change colour using any of the three methods explained opposite, but I recommend the following:
• Use the standing stitch method if the first stitch in the new colour is any of the basic stitches (dc, htr, tr).
• If you prefer not to use a standing stitch and the first stitch in the new colour is dc or ch-1, use the slip stitch method and then work 1 ch (the chain counts as the first dc or ch-1 of the new row).
• If the first stitch in the new colour is htr or a taller stitch, or a longer chain loop, use the incomplete stitch method and work the required number of chains to count as the first stitch.

ABBREVIATIONS

beg	beginning	FL	front loop	tog	together
BL	back loop	htr	half treble	tr	treble crochet
ch	chain		crochet	trtr	triple treble
dc	double crochet	sl st	slip stitch		crochet
dtr	double treble	sp(s)	space(s)	yo	yarn over
	crochet	st(s)	stitch(es)		

METHOD 1 – STANDING STITCH

Fasten off the old colour at the end of the row (or round), then use the new colour to start the new row with a standing stitch (see page 122). I prefer to use a standing stitch when changing colour because it provides a sturdier join and blends in nicely with the other stitches, making the colour join smoother. It does not create a gap at the edge of the work, which is especially useful if you don't plan to add a border to your blanket, and it is easier to discern when working the last stitch of the next row into the top of it.

It is preferable to have as few yarn cuts as possible, both for durability and so there will be fewer ends that might creep out later, but since you have to cut the yarn anyway when starting a new colour, it makes sense to choose the best option, even though rows worked in the same colour will start with turning chains. I recommend using a standing stitch to start each new round when working the borders, whether changing colour or not, to avoid creating an ugly bump or rib at the start of each round.

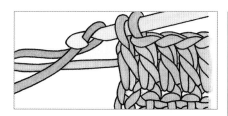

METHOD 2 – INCOMPLETE STITCH

Work the last stitch in the old colour up to the final 'yo, pull through'. Then wrap the new colour around the hook and use it to work the final 'yo, pull through' to complete the stitch. Use the new colour to work the required number of turning chains and continue along the row.

METHOD 3 – SLIP STITCH

Fasten off the old colour, then insert the hook into the stitch where you wish to make the join and work 'yo, pull through' with the new colour. Alternatively, place a slip knot on to the hook first, and pull the yarn through both the stitch and the slip knot. Then use the new colour to work the required number of turning chains and continue along the row.

WORKING OVER YARN ENDS

Whichever method you use to change colours, you can leave the cut tail ends of the yarn hanging at the back of the work and weave them in with a yarn needle after you finish your project. Alternatively, weave in the ends as you crochet along the next row by laying the tail ends behind the last row of stitches and working the next row of stitches over them. This reduces the amount of sewing at the end of your project.

MARRAKECH TECHNIQUE

For the mid-row colour changes on the Marrakech and Casablanca blankets (pages 32 and 68), use the incomplete stitch method, then continue along the row using the new colour. Do not cut the old colour, but leave it where it is.

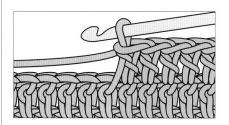

1 When you work back along the row, pick up the old colour and use the incomplete stitch method to change colours once more. This will leave a clearly visible vertical strand of yarn leading from the previous row to the stitch just completed at the changeover.

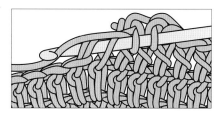

2 To make this vertical strand blend in, work the next tr as follows: yo, insert hook from right to left behind vertical strand and then into the next stitch of the row as normal, yo.

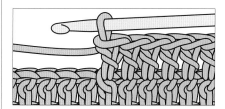

3 Pull a loop through both the stitch and the strand, then complete the tr as normal: [yo and pull through 2 loops on hook] twice.

CROCHET REFRESHER COURSE

Even experienced crocheters need their memories jogged from time to time. Whether you are a beginner or have been crocheting for years, these pages provide a handy reference guide to the key stitches and techniques.

Basic stitches

All crochet stitches are based on a loop of yarn pulled through another loop by a hook, repeated a different number of times to create stitches of different heights.

SLIP KNOT

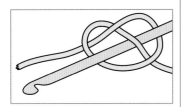

1 Make a loop of yarn and insert the crochet hook.

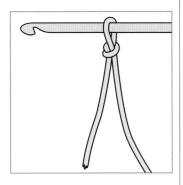

2 Gently pull on the short and long ends of yarn while holding the hook to create a slip knot.

⬭ CHAIN STITCH (CH)

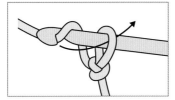

1 Make a slip knot as shown left. Wrap the yarn over the hook (or catch it with the hook) and pull it through the loop on the hook to make a new loop. One chain stitch (ch) made.

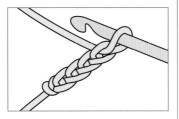

2 Repeat step 1 as required, moving your left hand every few stitches to hold the chain just below the hook.

● SLIP STITCH (SL ST)

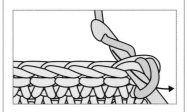

1 Insert the hook in the designated stitch (or space), wrap the yarn over the hook and pull a new loop through both the work and the loop on the hook. One slip stitch (sl st) made.

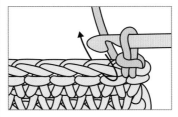

2 Repeat step 1 in each stitch to the end to complete one row of slip stitches.

✛ DOUBLE CROCHET (DC)

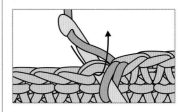

1 Insert the hook in the designated stitch (or space), wrap the yarn over the hook and pull a new loop through the work only.

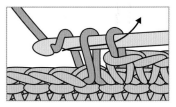

2 Wrap the yarn over the hook and pull a new loop through both loops on the hook.

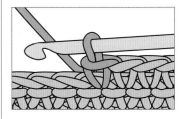

3 One loop remains on the hook. One double crochet stitch (dc) made. Repeat steps 1–2 in each stitch to the end to complete one row of double crochet stitches.

⊤ HALF TREBLE CROCHET (HTR)

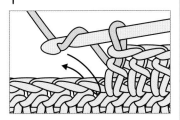

1 Wrap the yarn over the hook and insert the hook in the designated stitch (or space).

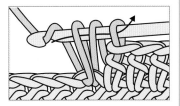

2 Pull a new loop through the work. You now have three loops on the hook. Wrap the yarn over the hook again. Pull through all three loops on the hook.

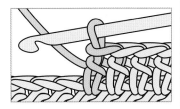

3 One loop remains on the hook. One half treble crochet stitch (htr) made. Repeat steps 1–2 in each stitch to the end to complete one row of half treble crochet stitches.

⊤ TREBLE CROCHET (TR)

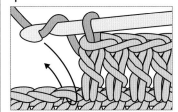

1 Wrap the yarn over the hook and insert the hook in the designated stitch (or space).

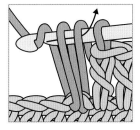

2 Pull a new loop through the work to make three loops on the hook. Wrap the yarn over the hook again. Pull a new loop through the first two loops on the hook.

3 Two loops remain on the hook. Wrap the yarn over the hook again. Pull a new loop through both loops on the hook.

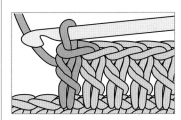

4 One loop remains on the hook. One treble crochet stitch (tr) made. Repeat steps 1–3 in each stitch to the end to complete one row of treble crochet stitches.

⊤ DOUBLE TREBLE CROCHET (DTR)

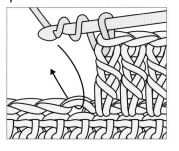

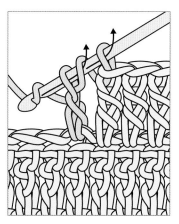

1 Wrap the yarn twice over the hook and insert the hook in the designated stitch (or space).

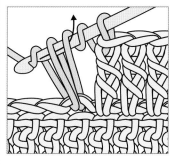

2 Pull a new loop through the work. You now have four loops on the hook. Wrap the yarn over the hook again and pull through the first two loops.

3 Three loops remain on the hook. Wrap the yarn over the hook and pull through the first two loops. Two loops remain on the hook. Wrap the yarn over again and pull through the two remaining loops.

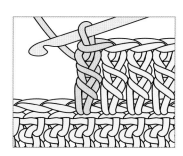

4 One loop remains on the hook. One double treble crochet stitch (dtr) made. Repeat steps 1–3 in each stitch to the end to complete one row of double treble crochet stitches.

⊤ TRIPLE TREBLE CROCHET (TRTR)

Work in the same way as double treble crochet, but start by wrapping the yarn over the hook three times instead of twice. Work off two loops at a time in the usual way.

Standing stitches

Chain stitches are usually used to form the first stitch of a new row or round. However, a standing stitch is my preferred method when working in rounds and when starting a new row in a new colour (see page 118 for more information).

STANDING DOUBLE CROCHET

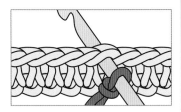

1 Make a slip knot on the hook and then insert the hook in the indicated stitch (or space).

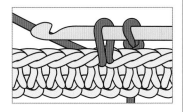

2 From here it is just like finishing a regular dc – yarn over, pull up a loop, yarn over and pull through both loops on the hook.

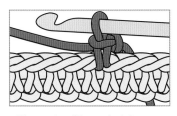

3 The stitch will have a little bump on the back (the initial slip knot). If you like, you can unravel this bump after completing the row or round; the stitch will stay secure.

STANDING TREBLE CROCHET – METHOD A

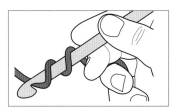

1 Wrap the yarn around the hook twice and secure these loops with a finger (this part can be a bit fiddly at first, but after a few times you will get the hang of it).

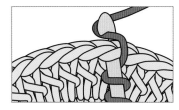

2 Insert the hook in the indicated stitch (or space) and pull up a loop.

3 From here it is like finishing a regular tr – [yarn over and pull through two loops] twice.

STANDING TREBLE CROCHET – METHOD B

1 Make a slip knot on the hook. (As with a standing dc, you can unravel the slip knot afterwards if you wish; the stitch will stay secure.)

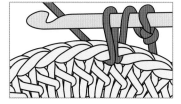

2 Yarn over and insert the hook in the indicated stitch (or space). Pull up a loop.

3 From here it is like finishing a regular tr – [yarn over and pull through two loops] twice.

VARIATIONS OF THE STANDING TREBLE CROCHET

If you have mastered the standing treble crochet, it is easy to make variations. For instance:

Standing tr cluster
If a pattern calls for a tr cluster as the first stitch, start by making a standing treble crochet, but don't finish it (just like you would not finish a regular tr when working a cluster). Now work the remaining stitches of the cluster and finish in the usual way.

Standing htr or standing dtr
For a standing htr, follow steps 1–2 of the standing tr (either method) and then yarn over and pull through all three loops on the hook. For a standing dtr, use the same technique as for the standing tr, but wrap the yarn over the hook three times (instead of twice).

Working into one loop only

The hook is usually inserted under both loops at the top of a stitch, but if it is inserted under just one loop, the empty loop creates a ridge on the front or back of the fabric. In this book, 'front loop' refers to the loop nearest to you and 'back loop' to the loop farthest from you, whether the right side or wrong side of the fabric is facing you.

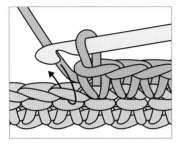 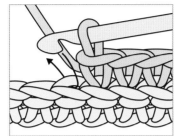

⌣ FRONT LOOP (FL)
If the hook is inserted under the front loop only, the empty back loop will show as a ridge on the other side of the work.

⌢ BACK LOOP (BL)
If the hook is inserted under the back loop only, the empty front loop creates a ridge on the side of the work facing you.

Post stitches

This technique creates raised stitches by inserting the hook around the post (stem) of the stitch, from the front or the back, instead of working under the loops at the top of the stitch.

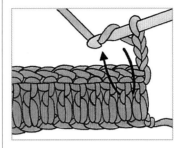 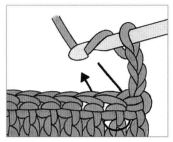

♂ FRONT POST (FP)
Work the stitch in the usual way, but insert the hook from the front to the back at the right of the next stitch, then bring it to the front again at the left of the same stitch.

♂ BACK POST (BP)
Work the stitch in the usual way, but insert the hook from the back to the front at the right of the next stitch, then take it to the back again at the left of the same stitch.

Decreases and clusters

Several stitches may be joined together at the top to decrease the total number of stitches. This can be denoted in the pattern using the abbreviation 'tog' along with the type and number of stitches – for example, tr3tog. Clusters are several stitches worked in the same place and joined together at the top – for example, 3-tr cluster. The method of joining the stitches together at the top is the same for both. To do this, work each stitch to be joined up to (but not including) the last 'yarn over and pull through'. One loop from each stitch will remain on the hook, plus the loop from the previous stitch. Yarn over once more and then pull a loop through all the loops on the hook to complete. Any number of any type of stitch can be worked together in a similar way.

ⓣ Puff stitch

A puff stitch is a cluster of half treble crohet stitches worked in the same place; a 3-htr puff is shown here.

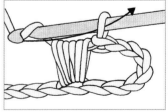 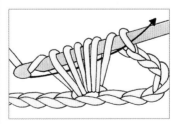

1 *Wrap the yarn over the hook, insert the hook where required and pull a loop through (3 loops on hook). Repeat from * twice more (7 loops on hook). Wrap the yarn over the hook and draw it through all seven loops.

2 Work an extra chain stitch at the top of the puff to complete the stitch.

Working in rounds

Most of the border designs in this book are worked in rounds, and throughout the patterns you will see the instruction 'join' at the end of a round. The most common way to join a round is with a slip stitch. However, another option is to close the round using a yarn needle; this is my preferred method because it gives an invisible join.

For some patterns the slip stitch join is absolutely fine – it will have less impact on a lacy pattern, for example. For other patterns – in general the more solid ones – a slip stitch will create a visible, less attractive join, so using a yarn needle to create a seamless join will create a much prettier, more polished result. Give both a try and then use whichever method you prefer for joining your rounds.

My preferred method for starting each new round is to use a standing stitch (see page 122), even when using the same yarn colour as the previous round, because it gives a seamless start to the round. However, you can use turning chains if you prefer (see page 118).

JOINING WITH A SLIP STITCH

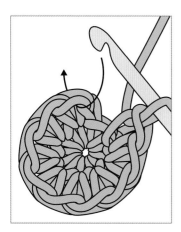

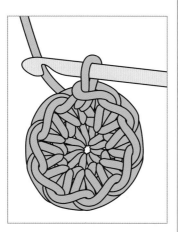

1 When you reach the end of the round, work a slip stitch into the top of the very first stitch of the round. If the next round is in a new colour, you can change colours by working this slip stitch in the new colour and then continue the next round in the new colour.

2 Here is the result. Remember that the slip stitch does not count as a stitch when working the next round.

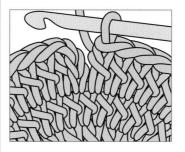

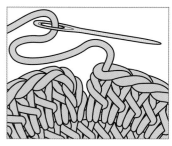

1 Complete the last stitch of the round. Cut the yarn, leaving a tail of about 10cm (4in).

2 Remove the hook from the last loop and pull the tail through the loop. Thread the tail on to a yarn needle.

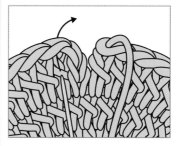

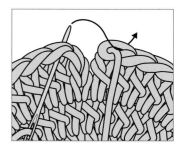

3 Insert the needle under both strands of the top V-shaped loop to the left of the first stitch (or beginning chain). Pull the yarn all the way through.

4 Insert the needle, from front to back, between the strands of the V-shaped loop at the top of the last stitch you worked (at the end of the round).

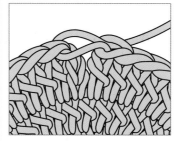

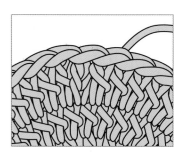

5 Pull the yarn through.

6 Adjust the tension of the yarn until the join is seamless. Weave in the end.

Finishing techniques

It is very easy to fasten off yarn when you have finished a piece of crochet, but do not cut the yarn too close to the work because you need enough yarn to weave in the end. It is important to weave in yarn ends securely so that they do not unravel. Do this as neatly as possible so that the woven yarn does not show through on the front of the work.

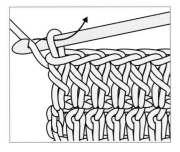

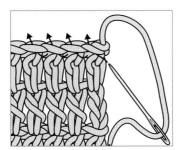

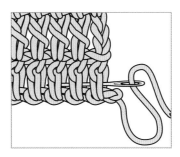

FASTENING OFF
To fasten off the yarn securely, work one chain and then cut the yarn at least 10cm (4in) away from the work. Pull the tail through the loop on the hook and tighten it gently.

WEAVING IN ENDS
To weave in a yarn end along the top or lower edge of a piece of crochet, start by threading the end on to a yarn needle. Take the needle through several stitches on the wrong side of the crochet, working stitch by stitch. Trim the remaining yarn. Make sure that you weave each yarn end through stitches of the same colour.

DOUBLE CROCHET SEAM
Use this technique to join two pieces of crochet together, such as the front and back panels of the Shiraz cushion (page 108). With right sides together, work a row of double crochet through both pieces together. You can work the stitches through both loops of each pair of stitches or just through the back (wrong-side) loops for a less bulky seam.

BLOCKING YOUR BLANKET

Most blankets need some blocking to let them shine. For lacy blankets in particular, I strongly recommend blocking to allow the pattern to really come out. Keep in mind that blocking will (slightly) enlarge the blanket, especially with those lacy patterns.

I use a simple yet effective method for blocking. Place the blanket on to a clean, soft underground, like a mattress, and gently tug it into the required shape with your hands. Then either spray the blanket with a water mister for plants and put a dry towel on top, or put a wet (but not soaking wet) towel on top.

If the blanket needs heavy blocking, I often put a couple of towels on top for extra weight.

Now simply let the blanket dry. If you feel it necessary, you can re-wet the towel or spray some extra water on to the blanket, to lengthen the blocking process (and thus make the effect even more sustainable). If the drying process takes too long for your liking, and the blanket is already in shape, simply remove the towel(s) from on top and allow it to dry like this.

Usually that should do the trick. However, if a blanket for some reason

is a bit wonky or uneven, you can call in extra help from pins. Either pin the whole blanket or just the area that is giving you trouble into the right shape. Then follow the same path as before, spraying the blanket with water or using a wet towel.

After washing the blanket, I recommend re-blocking. Spread out the blanket once again on a mattress or towel, gently pull it into the right shape, put one or more towels on top and allow it to dry.

FIND THE YARN

Here is a list of the yarns, colours and number of balls used to make the blankets and projects at the size shown in the photographs.

YARN DETAILS
- DMC Natura Just Cotton: 100% cotton, 155m (169yd) per 50g ball
- DROPS Belle: 53% cotton, 33% viscose, 14% linen, 120m (131yd) per 50g ball
- DROPS Paris: 100% cotton, 75m (82yd) per 50g ball
- Vinni's Colours Nikkim: 100% cotton, 119m (130yd) per 50g ball
- Yarn and Colors Fabulous: 50% cotton, 50% acrylic, 57m (62yd) per 50g ball

---

Blankets and borders

Marseille (page 12)
Vinni's Colours Nikkim:
- Scraps of yarn in multiple colours – 12 balls in total

Weimar (page 16)
Vinni's Colours Nikkim:
- Pale Blue-Green (518) – 2.1 balls
- Natural (500) – 3 balls
- Camel (504) – 1.5 balls
- Black (560) – 1.1 balls

Jaipur (page 20)
DROPS Paris:
- Light Light Pink (57) – 4 balls
- Medium Pink (33) – 8 balls
- Off White (17) – 2 balls
- Dark Grey (24) – 1 ball

Tokyo (page 24)
DMC Natura Just Cotton:
- Sable (N03) – 7 balls
- Blue Jeans (N26) – 0.3 ball
- Light Green (N12) – 0.3 ball
- Blé (N83) – 0.3 ball
- Spring Rose (N07) – 0.3 ball
- Glacier (N87) – 0.5 ball
- Lobelia (N82) – 0.5 ball

Havana (page 28)
DROPS Paris:
- Light Grey (23) – 1.3 balls
- Off White (17) – 1.3 balls
- Dark Beige (26) – 1.3 balls
- Light Ice Blue (29) – 1.3 balls
- Mustard (41) – 1.3 balls
- Dark Grey (24) – 1.3 balls

Marrakech (page 32)
Vinni's Colours Nikkim:
- Scraps of 521, 522, 525, 542, 557, 558, 562, 574, 575, 581, 582, 583 – 6 balls in total
- Black (560) – 1.5 balls
- Natural (500) – 1.5 balls

Bruges (page 36)
DMC Natura Just Cotton:
- Nacar (N35) – 4.5 balls

St George's (page 40)
Vinni's Colours Nikkim:
- Sunshine (535) – 4 balls
- Pale Sage (519) – 3.5 balls
- Natural (500) – 1.5 balls

Hanoi (page 44)
DROPS Paris:
- Off White (17) – 7 balls
- Light Mint Green (21) – 2 balls
- Light Old Pink (59) – 1.5 balls

Seoul (page 48)
DROPS Belle:
- Zinc (07) – 1 ball
- Silver (06) – 1 ball
- Beige (09) – 1 ball
- Light Blue (14) – 1 ball
- Brown (05) – 1 ball
- Off White (02) – 1 ball
- Dandelion (04) – 1 ball
- Light Beige (03) – 1 ball

Odessa (page 52)
DMC Natura Just Cotton:
- Acanthe (N81) – 1.2 balls
- Azur (N56) – 1.2 balls
- Rose Soraya (N32) – 2.4 balls (2 stripes)
- Tilleul (N79) – 1.2 balls
- Geranium (N52) – 1.2 balls
- Rose Layette (N06) – 1.2 balls
- Blé (N83) – 1.2 balls
- Blue Layette (N05) – 1.2 balls
- Blue Jeans (N26) – 1.2 balls

Lisbon (page 56)
DROPS Paris:
- Light Mint Green (21) – 8.5 balls
- Off White (17) – 7.5 balls

Istanbul (page 60)
DROPS Paris:
- Petrol (48) – 2 balls
- Dark Beige (26) – 2 balls
- Moss Green (25) – 1 ball
- Light Old Pink (59) – 4 balls
- Light Ice Blue (29) – 1 ball

Nairobi (page 64)
DMC Natura Just Cotton:
- Rose Layette (N06) – 2 balls
- Rose Soraya (N32) – 2 balls
- Lobelia (N82) – 2 balls
- Acanthe (N81) – 2 balls

Casablanca (page 68)
DROPS Paris:
- Scraps of yarn in multiple colours – 12 balls in total

Oslo (page 72)
DROPS Paris:
• Light Grey (23) – 5 balls
• Light Old Pink (59) – 2 balls
• Peach (27) – 1 ball
• Medium Pink (33) – 1 ball
• Light Pink (20) – 1 ball
• Dark Old Pink (60) – 1 ball

Stockholm (page 76)
DROPS Paris:
• Off White (17) – 2.5 balls
• Light Grey (23) – 2.5 balls
• Light Blue Purple (32) – 2.5 balls
• Petrol (40) – 2.5 balls
• Dark Grey (24) – 2.5 balls

St Petersburg (page 80)
DROPS Paris:
• Off White (17) – 4 balls
• Mustard (41) – 1 ball
• Dark Beige (26) – 1 ball
• Moss Green (25) – 1 ball
• Brown (44) – 1 ball

Buenos Aires (page 84)
DROPS Paris:
• Off White (17) – 8 balls
• Scraps of 02, 05, 11, 20, 21, 23, 26, 29, 30,
  33, 35, 38, 48, 58, 59 – 5 balls in total

Acapulco (page 88)
DROPS Paris:
• Black (15) – 4 balls
• Off White (17) – 4 balls
• Light Mint Green (21) – 2 balls

Borders (pages 95–100)
DMC Natura Just Cotton:
• Sable (N03)
• Ivory (N02)

Projects

Porto rug (page 104)
Hoooked RibbonXL (100% recycled fibres,
120m/131yd per 250g ball):
• Pearl White – 5 balls
• Scraps of Sweet Pink, Early Dew,
  Happy Mint, Iced Apricot, Frosted Yellow,
  Bubblegum Pink, Powder Blue, Sea Blue,
  Dark Grey, Light Grey – 7.6 balls in total

Chiang Mai potholder (page 106)
DROPS Paris:
• Mustard (41) or Light Blue Purple (32) –
  0.25 ball
• Light Pink (20) – 0.3 ball

Chiang Mai dish towel (page 106)
DROPS Paris:
• Off White (17) – 0.5 ball
• Light Pink (20) – 1 ball
• Light Blue Purple (32) – 0.25 ball
• Mustard (41) – 0.25 ball

Shiraz cushion (page 108)
DROPS Paris:
• Scraps of yarn in multiple colours –
  4.5 balls in total

Fez wall hanging (page 110)
• Made by Me XXL (super chunky-weight
  acrylic) in Off White – 1 ball
• Durable Glam (75% cotton, 25% polyester,
  130m/142yd per 50g ball) in Silver and
  Cream – 1 ball each
• Phildar Phil Sequins (100% polyester,
  130m/142yd per 25g ball) in Or – 0.25 ball

Salvador bedspread (page 112)
Yarn and Colors Fabulous:
• Cream (002) – 14 balls
• Pearl (043) – 10 balls
• Pastel Pink (046) – 10 balls
• Soil (028) – 10 balls
• Antique Pink (048) – 10 balls

Suppliers

We would like to thank the following companies
for generously supplying yarns to make the
blankets and projects in this book:

DMC Creative World
www.dmc.com

DROPS Design®

DROPS Design
www.garnstudio.com

ViNNiS COLOURS

Vinni's Colours
www.vinniscolours.co.za

Scaapi is a distributor of Vinni's Colours
and unique hand-dyed yarns.
www.scaapi.nl

YARN
AND
COLORS.

Yarn and Colors
www.yarnandcolors.com

INDEX

Credits

We would like to thank the yarn companies that generously supplied yarns for use in this book; see pages 126–127 for full details.

All photographs and illustrations are the copyright of Quarto Publishing plc. While every effort has been made to credit contributors, Quarto would like to apologise should there have been any omissions or errors – and would be pleased to make the appropriate correction for future editions of the book.

Author's acknowledgements

A big thanks to the people at Quarto for another lovely cooperation: Kate Kirby, Michelle Pickering (for making sense of all my notes…), Jackie Palmer, Moira Clinch, Danielle Watt, Cassie Lawrence and everybody else involved. Thank you Scaapi, Vinni's Colours, DROPS, DMC and Yarn and Colors for providing me with an abundance of the most beautiful yarns. I'm also grateful for the wonderful interaction with other crafters on Instagram and, of course, with the dear readers of this book. A last thank you goes to all the wonderful places in this stunning world that were the inspiration for the blanket designs.